In the Country Style

Timeless Designs for Today's Home

In the
Country Style

Timeless Designs for Today's Home

 Barbara Buchholz, Lisa Skolnik,
Robert Fitzgerald, Julie Fowler

MetroBooks

MetroBooks

An Imprint of the Michael Friedman Publishing Group, Inc.

Library of Congress Cataloging-in-Publication Data available upon request.

ISBN 1-56799-942-5

Editors: Susan Lauzau, Hallie Einhorn, and Francine Hornberger
Art Directors: Lynne Yeamans and Jeff Batzli
Designers: Lynne Yeamans, Meredith Miller, and Robbi Firestone
Photography Editors: Valerie Kennedy, Wendy Missan, Samantha Larrance, and Deidra Gorgos
Production Manager: Camille Lee
Introduction and *Italian Country* by Robert Fitzgerald; *French Country* by Barbara Bucholz and
Lisa Skolnik; *English Country* by Julie Fowler; *American Country* by Lisa Skolnik

Color separations by Colourscan Overseas Co. Pte. Ltd.
Printed in China by Leefung-Asco Printers Ltd

3 5 7 9 10 8 6 4 2

For bulk purchases and special sales, please contact:
Michael Friedman Publishing Group, Inc.
Attention: Sales Department
230 Fifth Avenue
New York, NY 10001
212/685-6610   FAX 212/685-3916

Visit our website:
www.metrobooks.com

Contents

INTRODUCTION

In today's speeding, whizzing, beeping, hurly-burly world of cell phones and modems and information overload, country life possesses an increasingly rare yet profoundly alluring quality of peacefulness. Country life has come to symbolize much more than just the "old-fashioned" rural lifestyle with which it was once associated. In fact, country life has become an antidote to the over-stimulating modern world. The slow cadence and serene rhythms of the countryside hold the key to a revitalized philosophy of life, a rediscovered way of living, a renewed pleasure in communing with others as well as with nature.

The notion of country life conjures vivid and powerful images in the mind's eye. Everyone has his or her own conception of what the ideal country setting would be, and no two conceptions are ever the same. These images are by nature very personal, etched by halcyon childhood memory or gleaned from a lifetime of travel and books and movies and magazines. Whatever their source, images of country life are unfailingly imbued with exalted themes of family, home, community, and nature. While country settings may vary widely, these themes prevail around the world.

A sprawling ranch in Montana, for example, does not appear to have much in common with a thatched-roof cottage in the English countryside, a lakeside pied-à-terre in Provence, a renovated monastery perched among Tuscan hills, or even the squat adobes found in the American Southwest. Yet the life that revolves around each of these settings is remarkably similar in tone and quality. Away from the hustle and bustle of the workaday world, the pace of life slows and, as the distractions of the modern world subside, time seems to flow backward. Nature once again regains its regal eminence. People interact on a more personal level. Above all, the value of a thing becomes more important than its worth. Removed from the à la carte amenities of urban and even suburban life, people come to appreciate things—material and other—for their intrinsic value, beauty, and ingenuity.

OPPOSITE: *Lemon yellow walls and a colorful assortment of china plates, bowls, and saucers imbue this English country dining room with a comforting sense of warmth and casualness. The natural blonde wood furnishings and framed advertisements hanging on the walls add to the rustic charm.*

ABOVE: *Dining al fresco is one of the grandest pleasures of Italian country living. This Tuscan pergola offers a perfect setting for whiling away an afternoon outdoors with family and friends eating a scrumptious pasta and drinking good wine.*

These themes of country life are reflected in the vernacular architecture and design of country dwellings. Most country architecture is intended to heighten the effect nature plays on the domestic experience. Large windows and porches, terraces and patios, porticoes and verandas are employed to bring the outdoors in and to integrate nature into the spaces used for dining and entertaining. When possible, the reverse is also true, and indoor activities are given some fresh air. Country folk get outside as often as possible to enjoy nature's many sounds, smells, and sights. Dining alfresco is a favorite pastime—tables and chairs can be arranged outside, or a picnic blanket can be thrown under a shady tree for an impromptu luncheon.

In a similar fashion, nature is celebrated in the choice of building materials used to construct country homes. Vernacular materials like wood, stone, and brick mirror the colors and textures of the landscape. Because of the integrity and earthiness of these indigenous materials, country homes seem to meld with the landscape and appear as old and noble as the land itself.

The sense of history that permeates country life is demonstrated in the ethnic and ancestral heritage of country furnishings. The furniture that populates today's country homes could have been found in similar dwellings several generations ago. These antiques are usually handmade and tend to have a primitive or naïve quality that reflects local customs and do-it-yourself dexterity or even a specific artisan tradition. They are built of heavy, coarse wood that is distinctly less ornate than more sophisticated, finely carved antiques with more pedigreed origins. Nevertheless, these pieces are well crafted and solidly constructed. Today their natural or brightly painted surfaces have been weathered and worn to an evocative patina. As the country style has become more and more appealing, contemporary craftsmen and furniture makers have produced country collections that share this sense of enduring quality.

ABOVE: *The best country kitchens integrate modern technology into a traditional design scheme. This kitchen in Provence, for example, has a fine stainless steel stove and oven and all the latest in modern cooking convenience, but these appliances complement the room's country décor.*

RIGHT: *The focal point of a renovated barn, this family room is distinguished by the exquisite craftsmanship and sturdy building materials that are hallmarks of the most compelling country homes. Broad, rough-hewn floor boards, intricate wainscoting, and antique, beveled-glass windows are a few of the design elements that testify to the quality of rural, turn-of-the-century American handiwork.*

The serene comforts and quietude of the country home offer an alternative to the frenetic modern world. Technology holds little sway over the best country retreats. After all, truly getting away means leaving behind the computer and the cell phone. A sense of community is created, therefore, not by installing satellite dishes or by going online, but by designing living spaces to accommodate large gatherings of family and friends. Nothing epitomizes country hospitality like the oversized dining table, which is typically made of heavy, coarse wood that has been scratched and nicked and worn smooth over time by the vicissitudes of daily life. Hearths or wood-burning stoves provide warmth in the most rustic country homes and offer another place for family and friends to congregate.

True country style is much more than a decorating trend. On a more significant level it is the embodiment of a lifestyle, the physical expression of a state of mind. In many ways the architecture and design reflect the personal values of fortitude, honesty, integrity, and strength that life in the country represents. So whether the house is located in the far reaches of a remote countryside or right in the teeming gridlock of the city, the style itself can have a transforming effect on the life it adorns. Country style is imbued with the spirit of a gentle, slower-paced time and a heightened awareness of personal values. The style is simple and unaffected, cozy and comfortable, casual and informal. It brings together the best of the old with the finest of the new in an eclectic mix of the urban and the rural, the pioneering and the colonial, the rugged and the refined. It can be sophisticated and contemporary, or it can be more traditional. In whatever form it takes, country style reflects an enduring theme that will remain popular as modern life progresses further and further from its country origins.

A B O V E : *This English sitting room's many windows, clean structural lines, and uncluttered décor add to the feeling of space and openness, which are cherished aspects of country design.*

The timeless quality of country design is equally apparent in other home furnishings. Homespun fabrics and quilts have plain weaves and textures and are vegetable-dyed in earthy colors or woven in miniature prints. Treasured heirloom linens reveal a reverence for the past as well as for the artisan tradition. Hand-thrown pottery and other indigenous crafts and folk art also reflect the unpretentious charm of country life.

O P P O S I T E : *While this French country bedroom set is more sophisticated than common country furnishings, the layout of the room suggests a casual and relaxed sensibility.*

Part One

FRENCH COUNTRY

INTRODUCTION

Nothing conjures up the notion of French country style more vividly than the vignettes that have been etched in our memories over the years, gleaned from sources as varied as our travels, foreign films, restaurants, and the works of renowned artists.

Sometimes, just one element is enough to immediately suggest French country design. Picture a pair of handmade white lace curtains that cover multipaned windows through which bright sunlight streams from an azure sky. Or, imagine a Louis XV walnut armchair with hand-carved slats and woven rush seats. An imposing armoire with paneled double doors and intricate carvings covering its richly burnished cherry exterior also conveys a French impression.

In other instances, the effect is carried out by an entire roomful of elements that work together to embody the French country mood. Envision a large country kitchen with colorful tiles hiding crusty stone walls, a long wooden harvest table surrounded by mismatched chairs, an antique cooker adjacent to a working fireplace providing physical warmth, and an array of copper pots suspended from a ceiling rack and gleaming overhead. A living room graced with a magnificent old hearth, worn ceiling beams, and a stone floor can exude an equally classic French ambience, particularly when the upholstery consists of tiny provincial prints.

The best part about French country style is that no single ideal truly defines it. France is the only country in Western Europe that belongs to both the northern and southern portions of the continent, resulting in a wide diversity of design and architectural elements. Each of the provinces, and even many of the towns within a particular province, has its own colloquial style. All these regional characteristics contribute to the common vernacular that has come to be known as French country style.

In Brittany, a northwestern province popular for country getaways, old houses in myriad configurations (from small manors—the two-room dwellings dating from the sixteenth century that first allowed a family and its domestics to have their own spaces—to farmhouses and row houses built to house several families around communal fields) are constructed from indigenous granite and topped with tufted thatch. In Normandy, just northwest of Paris, charming half-timbered structures

OPPOSITE: *The Rhone river flows through the gentle landscape of southeastern France, making it a fertile farming region. Among the region's crops is lavender, which lends its evocative scent to perfume.*

Provence, perhaps most famous as the standard bearer of the French country style, is located in the southeastern portion of France, and its homes exude a Mediterranean flavor. The exteriors of limestone rubble structures are smoothed down and drenched in earth tones that reflect the cheerful countryside. Produced from oxides in the local sand and rocks, such hues as rose, ocher, wisteria, and sienna adorn the otherwise plain façades and are punctuated by contrasting colors used on the shutters. Over time, the sun bleaches the colors to more subdued tones.

Inside the abodes, local construction styles are equally distinct, for they are highly dependent on the modest materials native to the particular region. Although many of these architectural elements were originally designed primarily with the intention of providing structural support, they also serve as stunning decorative details. For instance, a beamed and trussed ceiling is a breathtaking sight that radiates old-world charm, but such a ceiling was actually designed because it offered the sturdiest and most sensible construction technique. The joists and supports were traditionally crafted of local timber, with many retaining their natural curves since entire trees sometimes were used at one time. The treatment of the timbers varied by region; some were left natural, while others were whitewashed or stained with walnut oil for a richer look.

Fireplaces and hearths, which served as the original center of the home because they were used for heating the household and cooking, also reflect regional differences. Some were built with niches set into the wall to provide extra storage; others had benches off to one side for resting by the fire. The most imposing were built in dressed stone, though most were constructed of simple rubble, which ages gracefully.

Walls were constructed of the same materials as the exterior of a structure. They could be timbered and filled in with lime or mud plaster, or they could be made of brick. Floors often consisted of flagstones or brick in northern France and clay tiles in the South.

ABOVE: *Much of the charm of French country style lies in the attention to detail that is so typical. Here, potted plants and a window box bring warmth and color to the façade of an ivy-draped home, while sunshine peeks through the lace-curtained second-story window.*

faced with clay and punctuated with steeply sloped roofs prevail. In Alsace, at the far northeastern border of the country, the same materials have been used to produce houses that are heavily ornamented with colorful hues and gingerbread trims, reminiscent of nearby Germany.

To the south, the same kind of diversity reigns supreme. Large whitewashed dwellings with canal-tiled roofs dot the Basque landscape in the western part of the region. These homes were often built three stories tall to house a cart shed on the first floor, the living quarters on the second floor, and a balconied attic, where harvests were stored and clothes were hung to dry in the open air, on the top level.

LEFT: *The past is ever present at this warm-hued Alsatian farm-house, where a creative gardener has transformed an old well into a unique planter, brimming with colorful blooms.*

TOP: *Plentiful and enduring, limestone was a major building material in the south of France. Here, in the town of St. Jeannet, a doorway dating to 1834 is set into the limestone façade.* ABOVE: *A delightful farmhouse in Normandy features the half-timbered construction and thatched roof that are so typical of this region.*

Just as the architectural components of various regions are distinct, so too are the furnishings, though they bear striking similarities in their general forms and functions. There are a couple of aspects that account for the parallels. First, French country furnishings were made,

primarily, to serve specific needs that people throughout France shared. Thus, the same types of pieces are found throughout all the regions, though these pieces differ in ornamentation.

Second, the styles that slowly seeped into the provinces where working-class people lived came from the same sources—the courts of such design tastemasters as King Louis XIII and King Louis XV (the latter having had the greatest impact on French country design). As styles traveled to the different regions after decades of popularity among the wealthy, they were slightly altered to suit the particular climate, geography, and financial resources.

Thus, a *dressoir* (a buffet topped with rows of shelves) would be decorated in a spare manner if it was made in Auvergne in central France, but would have intricately carved details if it were crafted in Normandy. In Brittany, turned spindle plate guards would embellish shelves, while painted flowers would enhance an Alsatian piece. Beds were totally enclosed by richly carved wooden panels in Brittany, semi-boxed and hung with drapes in Normandy, and made with four short posts, then draped with canopies, in the South.

Further differences in style arose from the preferences of individual craftsmen, how much or how little embellishment they favored, and their degree of skill. In fact, it is the individual interpretations and the odd or eclectic details that worked their way into country pieces, rather than any literal copying of high styles, that give French country furnishings their true charm and charisma.

Today, the French country look is coveted for its casual elegance and originality. Ironically, though, this much beloved style defies the notion of decorating as we know it, since it evolved, for the most part, from working-class roots. Many individual pieces may be quite magnificent and grand, but these were often commissioned for special occasions, such as weddings, where specific pieces were given as part of a dowry. Granted, as the population living in the countryside became more affluent in the nineteenth cenury, more pieces were made and the trappings of decor, such as wall and floor treaments, became more

ABOVE: *Roofs of terra-cotta tiles characterize the venerable dwellings found in the oldest section of this quintessential Provençal town.*

refined. But this is a style that evolved from the realities of country life, and as such does not need to be strictly confined.

Thus, bringing the French country style into our homes does not require a perfect duplication of the elements, for there were few, if any, hard and fast rules to begin with. Furthermore, every single element need not be ostensibly French country. An individual piece—be it a distinguished French armoire or simple harvest table—can work beautifully with furnishings from other countries as well as with traditions that are older or more modern.

In the following pages, we will examine the individual components and rooms that best define the French country style, as well as the exteriors and their settings. Each of these aspects has the almost magical power to create a mood that unmistakably spells *la belle France.*

THE OUTSIDE VIEW

Throughout France, the homes and landscaping reflect the geography, climate, and natural resources of the province in which they are situated. Hence, the regional, or vernacular, designs that have emerged over time are as distinct in France as they are in the United States, where narrow townhouses rise vertically in the urban centers of the Northeast to compensate for the scarcity of land and where mansions with immense porches proliferate in the deep reaches of the South.

In rural areas of Normandy, where wood has traditionally been plentiful, timber-framed buildings are commonplace. In Brittany, modest farmers would construct thatched or stone houses, which they shared with family members and animals. Wooden chalets with sloping roofs were designed to protect occupants and the structures themselves from heavy rains in the mountainous Alps. And in Provence, inhabited long ago by Romans, clay tile roofs in different hues have dotted the landscape for centuries.

At the same time, similarities have abounded and continue to be present. Throughout France, in both cities and the countryside, home-owners share a deep love for their abodes and pay great attention to the choice of architectural details, such as the windows, doors, and trim, as well as to the colors used to enhance the façades. They eagerly call upon their own skills or those of their area's craftspeople—the thatcher, brick maker, stone mason, carpenter, and gardener—to make the exteriors of their homes as enticing as the interiors.

OPPOSITE: *The rough-cut stone street and the half-timbered home with a brick foundation are typical of Normandy, where the wooded countryside traditionally offered a rich source of timber for construction. Sometimes the timbers were laid in a diagonal display to show the craftsperson's skill and artistic bent. Thatched roofs, once common, gave way to slate in the nineteenth century, as slate was sturdier, more fire-resistant, and provided a more dignified demeanor.*

LEFT: *French country cottages often put on a painted face. Their owners either completely cover the surface of the structure with pigment, or simply focus on the building's prominent architectural elements, making them even more eye-catching by painting them in bright hues. Here, cream-colored limestone bricks are left in their natural state, but the characteristic Mediterranean windows and doors, which tend to be narrow, deep, and flanked by slat-board shutters, are painted a clean sky blue. Red and pink flowers, lush foliage, and lace curtains are additional characteristically French elements.*

RIGHT: *In Nice, homes are painted brilliant colors with pigments made from local rocks. The paints not only dazzle the eyes, but waterproof the exteriors as well. With deep crimson walls and turquoise blue louvered wooden doors, this home is a vivid example. The white frames around the doors and the lacy wrought-iron detailing, which has a Spanish feeling, make the crimson and blue even more prominent. With time and sunlight, the bright colors will weather to a softer palette.*

OPPOSITE: *There are many ways in which the French introduce a welcoming feeling to the home. In this case, the feat is accomplished by trellised plants climbing along the window-framed front door, two pots housing rose bushes that add color and fragrance, and foliage that softens the brick walkway. But the handmade lace curtains, known as* dentelle, *make the strongest statement by inviting onlookers to behold the home within, rather than by shielding it from view.*

RIGHT: *Gargoyles such as this can be seen on churches in the French countryside, as well as on some grand country homes that sport Gothic styling. Although they appear to be nothing more than fanciful embellishments, gargoyles were actually designed to serve as practical drainage spouts. These fantastic figures were thought to embody fallen angels who were being given a second chance to redeem themselves by guarding buildings. The action of water rushing through their spouts was said to wash away evil.*

RIGHT: *Stone houses dating back centuries are found in the celebrated wine-producing area of Bordeaux. Here, a stately home rests atop the hill, its unadorned façade emphasizing its simple grandeur. Nestled into the hillside below is a smaller cottage-style residence, graced with exuberant foliage and vines. Adding a sense of warm welcome is a planter bursting with colorful blooms set upon the wrought-iron balcony.*

LEFT: *Already flanked by old white shutters and luxurious leafy vines, the windows in this master's house, or* maison de maître, *are given an additional decorative boost by window boxes filled with vibrant bougainvillea. A skillful use of dark and light materials provides soft contrast between the roof, graced with tiny dormers, and the commanding stonework.*

RIGHT: *Located in a small village, this stone house was built close to its neighbors, a tradition that developed partly because of space constraints and also for security reasons. Stone was always favored over timber when available, and the irregular sizes and shapes—no two stones alike—lend an air of individuality.*

OPPOSITE: *Breton blue, a favorite color in Brittany because of the area's many boating and fishing activities, is used on the shutters, window trim, front door, and wooden gate of this home. Only a side door boasts a deep brick red. Both hues enhance the exterior by enlivening the whitewashed façade.*

Getting away from the big city and finding refuge in the country is just as much a French phenomenon as it is an American one, and the choice of weekend abodes takes many forms. For example, a tiny half-timbered Alsatian house (RIGHT) set deep in the woods offers the desired change of pace with its sloping roofline and the privacy provided by its massive stone walls set with relatively few small windows. Another family's preferred getaway is a small stone cottage in Auvergne (BELOW). Quaint dormered windows, stones bearing different hues, and a secluded location create the appeal of this retreat.

ABOVE: *Espaliers have long been a popular gardening device, creating wonderful decorative effects within a fairly small amount of space. From a central vertical stem attached to the wall of a house, branches are trained to grow sideways in tidy rows. Sometimes, the branches yield apples and pears, other times fragrant flowers. Here, an espalier growing against the side wall of a brick home fans out its greenery and red bouquets of color.*

ABOVE: *Whether stopping for a drink at a Parisian café or relaxing at a country home, the French favor taking their meals outdoors, capturing the best view for enjoyment. Here is proof that they know how to set as elegant a table in the fresh outdoors as they do within their homes. All they need are favorite candlesticks, white china, simple crystal, and light-toned linens.* Bon appetit.

ABOVE: *Though the walls were constructed from rough stone, which has been washed with a pale yellow hue, and the door was made of crude wood, the owners of this barn still felt it impor-tant to leave a personal touch by carving a tiny heart in one door panel and fronting it with an exuberant garden of tulips and lilacs.*

RIGHT: *Grapes are an important crop in France, and the process of producing wine is a time-consuming labor. In spring new vines are planted; in summer they are tended; and in autumn the grapes are picked, crushed, and fermented. Just as no two grapes are alike, neither are two "high houses," or* maisons en hauteur, *prevalent in the provinces where wine is made. These centuries-old structures were designed to have the upstairs serve as living quarters, while the ground level would serve as a wine store. Originally a Mediterranean innova-tion, the style quickly caught on in Burgundy, Provence, and Languedoc.*

RIGHT: *In Provence, a palette of warm, earthy hues made from the oxides in the local sand are used to embellish the homes. Shutters and trims are often painted in contrasting colors, and the overall effect is both picture-pretty and quite polished despite the simplicity of the structures. Here is a perfect example of the magic wrought by this practice: with just a piece of faience and a simple lace shawl, a cottage in Provence looks elegantly turned out thanks to its already exquisite façade.*

Multipaned windows that extend down to the
floor but are used like doors to gain access
to or exit from a room are known as French
windows and can be dressed up or down to suit
a residence. The windows on a countryside
chateau in France (ABOVE) *sport louvered doors,*
while those on a limestone farmhouse (RIGHT) *are*
framed with rustic slat shutters. In either case,
flowers add a great deal of charm to the façade.

LEFT AND ABOVE: *Many farmhouses in the provinces were built of limestone rubble, with granite framing stones and simple wood plank shutters and doors. Such drab materials left residences looking quite somber, a situation easily remedied in summer months with foliage. With the addition of simple boxes filled with flowers, these two farmhouses in Auvergne go from pallid to picturesque.*

LEFT: *Renaissance-style carvings are found on manors and religious monuments throughout lower Brittany, where granite was frequently used to build homes. Here the moldings and jambs are still perfectly intact on a sixteenth-century Breton manor, framing a massive oak door that was the standard of the day (it was supplanted by framed versions in the seventeenth century). While the dusty red hue seems like an authentic touch, the door was a rich honey color when it was first built and was repainted to suit twentieth-century taste.*

LEFT, TOP: *In Normandy, windows boasting two rows of small panes typically appear in pairs with a structural post dividing them. Thanks to such detailing, they are charming in their own right. In this half-timbered house, the windows need no further adornment than a mass of red flowers.*

LEFT, BOTTOM: *With its swirling lines and heart-shaped designs, this wrought-iron gate creates a welcoming entrance filled with old-fashioned charm. A delicate praying angel offers a sense of reassurance, as she seems to keep watch over those within the farmhouse. Further evidence of hospitality is seen in the house number, which has been lovingly stenciled in blue and white to stand out against the gray stone and hence can be seen easily by visitors.*

RIGHT: *Home sweet home. At the end of a long gravel driveway lined with shade-providing trees, the sight of home—in this case a turreted château, the French equivalent of a large country home—is a welcome visage.*

ROOMS FOR LIVING

While the archetypal French country living room of today is a charming space outfitted with all the right trappings, it is actually a rather recent innovation. Until the nineteenth century, many French living quarters (save for the communal abodes that sheltered multigenerational families in parts of southern and eastern France) consisted of only one or two rooms.

The one room that these homes were sure to have was the *salle*, which served as a sort of kitchen-cum–living room. All the activities of a household—from cooking and eating to gathering around the fire and sleeping—took place in the *salle*. If a home was divided into two rooms, the second was a sparsely furnished bedroom, or *chambre*, which was often located to the side of the *salle* or under the eaves of the attic.

Yet despite the limited number of rooms, many newly restored cottages and farmhouses in France sport stunning living rooms, loaded with architectural details and striking pieces of furniture that reflect the provincial style. So where did these special spaces come from?

Most were once living quarters for the family livestock. Households kept their valuable animals on the ground floors of their homes and lived either above them or off to one end of the structure. As animals were slowly evicted from these spaces, the rooms underwent a series of upgrades until they ended up as the sort of living rooms we know today. Other living rooms (especially those with hearths) originated as *salles* and were converted to their present incarnations when a contemporary kitchen was added on to the home.

The architectural elements of these rooms—beamed ceilings, timbered fittings, and stone floors—have been somewhat refurbished to ensure structural safety but have been left primarily intact to retain their rustic charm. Massive limestone hearths, which were often hidden behind newer walls as cottages were modernized over the years, have been unearthed, restored, and enhanced with every sort of fireplace accessory. Although these spacious rooms are not always filled

OPPOSITE: *There is no need to sacrifice high style in the French countryside. Here, simple pieces are paired together for a country version of Empire styling, exuding the same sort of symmetrical balance and glamour found in that type of decor. But the vignette also retains an aura of earthiness thanks to the cunning way in which design elements of the Empire period, such as gilt trim and yellow walls, have been manipulated; gilt is seen here only in small doses (on the mirror, the pulls of the commode, and the rims of the topiary pots), and the walls are mellow instead of bold.*

with strictly provincial furnishings, they certainly include enough of these kinds of pieces to create a French country ambience.

Achieving this look in a contemporary room can be as simple as incorporating a massive provincial armoire, some lace curtains, or a few Louis XV–inspired banquettes into the decor. Or, the architectural bones of a room can be manipulated to create the desired mood. Installing a French country–style beamed ceiling, a large stone hearth with copper accessories, or a tiled floor will do the trick. Regardless of which route is chosen, the result will be the same: the room will be imbued with classic French country charm.

BELOW: *Like a crusty old cauldron brimming with all sorts of tasty ingredients, this antiquated space is filled with a wide range of appealing pieces. Shapely and light, these pieces cast their sunny dispositions upon the room, preventing the massive dark Gothic architecture from making the space seem archaic. A blue fleur-de-lis pattern stenciled on the chalk white walls, along with checkered upholstery in the same shades, provides a cheery counterpoint to the dank-looking limestone cornices and hearth and gives the space its French country spark.*

ABOVE: *Since a hearth is the heart of many a French home, clever decorating devices were enlisted to suggest a fireplace in this country living room. Now a stylized version, complete with a faux mantel created by cornice molding, is the focal point of the space. But it is actually the matched pair of classic eighteenth-century settees, complete with rush seats, that gives the room its French country aura. Pillows and curtains made out of traditional Provençal fabrics (patterned after the printed cottons originally imported to France from India in the seventeenth century) and a Kashmir shawl covering the coffee table further imbue the room with unusual authenticity.*

OPPOSITE: *Since hearths are such an important and beautiful part of regional style in France, country kitchens are often turned into living rooms when homes are rehabbed. Here, a typical fireplace in Brittany, which was clearly once the functional center of a kitchen, has become the dramatic focal point of a sitting room. The hearth is surrounded by a hodgepodge of local pieces collected by the homeowners, and it is warmed up with a new floor that boasts a traditional pattern, covering the cold antiquated flagstones underneath.*

ABOVE: *A once humble country space becomes a bit more highbrow by playing on its natural attributes. The imposing open fireplace, edged with dressed stones, used to be the center of the original kitchen before the space was transformed into a living room. Now surrounded by pieces that have a polished country appeal, such as a posh winged chair, a sumptuous sofa, and a gleaming ladder-back chair, the fireplace takes on an air of grandeur.*

LEFT: *A cavernous living room in an old country home in France becomes downright cozy thanks to an array of French antiques that come from a variety of periods. An ornate eighteenth-century marble mantel and a gilt mirror anchor the room while helping to cut the ceiling height down to size. Meanwhile, a whimsical play on symmetry draws the eye toward such fabulous matching decorative elements as the torchères, sconces, Deco chairs, and pieces of pottery, thereby diverting attention away from the excess of space and rendering the setting more intimate.*

RIGHT: *Do not be deceived by the apparent simplicity of a country tableau. Here, the chalky white tones of a coarse plaster wall and rugged hearth are enriched by a seemingly casual, but actually carefully planned, arrangement of accents in rich hues of blue. The accessories, which include refined pieces of Chinoiserie pottery, rustic seascapes, and a modest wood chair, strike just the right balance to give the setting a polished but still provincial appeal.*

RIGHT: *A mantel in a modest French country cottage goes from mundane to magnificent when it is used as a topiary form. The gilt-edged mirror and matching urns add a touch of glamour to the setting, balancing the earthy ambience prompted by the foliage and lending an air of elegance to the funky approach.*

LEFT: *An innovative use of pattern is responsible for the casual yet cosmopolitan elegance of this living room in the South of France. While the scheme appears at first glance to be quite bold and forthright, it actually demonstrates subtle variations, for there are different types of stripes on the sofa, chairs, and walls. As these elements play off one another, they create the illusion of cohesiveness.*

ABOVE: *Although this living room in a French country home sports all the touches of a formal decor, the features have been relaxed a bit to fit the locale. The damask sofa is overstuffed enough to be comfortably casual, while a typical Provençal cotton print makes a stately Louis XV bergère seem less intimidating and far more inviting. A traditional soft yellow hue warms up the entire space.*

ABOVE: *Provincial furnishings were made by anonymous craftsmen in every region of France, often reflecting the distinctive styles of their period. But precise dating is difficult because some forms, such as the domed cherry Louis XV armoire in this sitting room, were popular and continued to be made in the provinces long after the specific style fell out of favor in Parisian workrooms. As this cabinet clearly shows, a piece of this scale can have a major impact on an entire room.*

RIGHT: *The adventurous use of color can make a traditional space seem far more engaging. Here, deep azure, the shade of the sky right after sunset, gives a sense of drama to what is for the most part a fairly traditional country room. Another novel touch is the mixing of contemporary pieces with such French provincial elements as classic ladder-back armchairs, Empire fauteuil, and a Regency corner cabinet.*

RiGHT: *Sometimes, just one powerful detail can imbue a room with a specific flavor. These vibrant curtains made of a hand-blocked Provençal cotton give a huge dose of French country styling to a plain window in a city apartment. Coupled with a simple metal window box filled with flowers of a similar hue, the curtains help to create a vignette that is far more dynamic than the individual components.*

Regardless of pedigree, when similar objects are
gathered together en masse, the sum is greater
than the parts. Here, two tableaux from French
country homes—one created from ordinary vases
filled with freshly cut flowers (LEFT) and the
other from antique decanters and a tea caddy
(ABOVE)—illustrate the point. Despite the fact
that they are in the midst of rustic surroundings,
these vignettes demonstrate the chic savoir faire
for which the French are renowned. Both settings
are bathed in sunny yellow, a color that not only
has a history of tradition in the French countryside, but can add warmth and depth to any style
of room.

LEFT: *The travails that befall a structure in the French countryside are rarely repaired; instead, these imperfections become prized parts of the decor. Thus, the missing paneling from a limestone hearth and the damaged area above a door frame where a cornice once rested are seen as signs of character rather than as shortcomings. Together, they contribute to the ambience and integrity of the residence.*

RIGHT: *The nooks and crannies of this secretary have been mined to display a charming collection of Limoges boxes, plus a few larger pieces of traditional tole. While these classics are right at home on the Louis XVI piece, virtually any antique desk or cabinet can acquire a French country tone when accessorized with provincial collectibles.*

LEFT: *Formal French furnishings can be equally at home in the countryside. Here, a Louis XV sofa, covered with pillows inspired by Aubusson tapestries, anchors a distinctly Victorian living room in a country home. The piece works well with the eclectic elements of the room, which range from floridly romantic statues of angels to Gothic Revival lamps.*

ABOVE: *Reproduction fabrics and furnishings can be used to evoke a French country feeling. The flowery print of this chintz was inspired by the prints of Provence, while the detailing of the carved armoire takes its cues from the provincial pieces of the eighteenth century.*

The trappings of grand country living, such as intricate wall treatments,
elaborate hearths, and beautiful wood and stone floors, take center stage in
these living rooms in the French countryside. Although one room (RIGHT) is
purely Louis XV and the other (ABOVE) is a romantic milieu that borrows from
many periods, both spaces contain fine examples of French antiques. But
thanks to the comfortably lived-in looks of the furnishings and the obvious
signs of wear and tear on the hearths, the rooms also radiate rustic spirit.
Like elegant outfits that should be worn instead of stored away in a closet,
lavish spaces seem far less pretentious when they are used every day.

THE COMMUNAL KITCHEN

Throughout French history, good food and drink have been raised to the level of art, which is why the kitchen has been not only a place to prepare meals, but a forerunner of today's heart-of-the-home room. Here, food is prepared, meals are savored, and people join together for sustenance of both the spirit and stomach.

Because the communal kitchen has traditionally served all these functions—and still does today—it has needed to include areas for cooking and cleaning as well as for eating and gathering. Whether these spaces remain distinct or are melded together depends to a large degree on the room's square footage.

Stylistically, there is great latitude in the choice of materials, colors, and design styles. However, the architecture of the home, the furnishings used in other rooms, and the age-old traditions passed down through the various provinces provide the greatest incentive for one kitchen to take on the charm of a Brittany farmhouse and another the splendor of a Loire Valley château.

Several features appear more frequently and have become almost trademarks of the French communal kitchen. A working fireplace was originally an essential because it provided the home's main source of heat. Today, many homes still have a large hearth—sometimes functional, sometimes decorative—as well as a mantel and walk-in–size alcove.

Generous storage is also characteristic of the French country kitchen. Pieces range from richly carved *dressoirs, vaisseliers* (cabinets or dressers with shelves), *buffets-bas* (waist-high cupboards used as sideboards), *panetières* (intricately shaped and carved cupboards for storing bread), and armoires down to simple slabs for shelves and unadorned cabinets. Some owners prefer to keep everything within view; others like to conceal the contents.

A large table and comfortable seating are critical elements for eating and lingering in the communal kitchen. The most common setup consists of an unadorned rectangular wooden farmhouse-style table surrounded by rush-bottomed ladder-back chairs, appearing sometimes in an assortment of styles.

OPPOSITE: *Knowing the superb culinary skills of the French, it is easy to understand why they have tradtionally coveted copper pots. Most households had collections of such cookware, which would be hung on racks because storage space was minimal. Arrayed in this manner, the pots were out of the way yet always within reach.*

Rustic earthy materials—the most popular being brick, wood, stone, and terra-cotta—are used in a variety of shapes and sizes to line kitchen walls, floors, and countertops. These elements offer age-old elegance as well as practicality.

And last but not least, pot racks (known as *crémaillères*) are integral components of the communal kitchen, having had a long and fruitful history in the French countryside. Along with the requisite copper pots that dangle from them, these highly practical elements also make beautiful, gleaming decorative accessories.

RIGHT: *This contemporary kitchen pays clever and indisputable homage to French country styling. The hard-wearing black-and-white tile floor, laid in a bold diamond pattern, is linoleum instead of clay, and the requisite baker's rack has been replaced by high-tech stainless steel industrial shelves to provide open storage. But the most prized elements of the French country kitchen remain perfectly intact, such as pots suspended from the ceiling and burnished walls rubbed with an earthy-colored hue.*

RIGHT: *A kitchen emanating a French country feeling does not necessarily have to sport anything specifically French in style. Here, a British Aga cooker, which heats food as well as the home's water system, serves as an anchor. Displays of pots and dried flowers lend a true country feeling to the space. But the ornately patterned tiles used in the backsplash, along with a set of intricately embellished chairs caned in colored stripes, give the kitchen the kind of panache that says French country.*

ABOVE: *Prized copper pots hang like medals on a wall in this French country kitchen, which boasts an elegant hodgepodge of furnishings achieved through years of tasteful, and heartfelt, accumulating. The wood pieces warm up the flagstone floor and contrast with the intricately enameled cast-iron wood-burning stove traditionally used for warming winter soups and stews. Note the elegant glasses and decanter on the table, which show that entertaining is one of the many activities that take place in this multifaceted room.*

OPPOSITE: *Thanks to similarities in shape, scale, and condition, a medley of ruggedly disparate pieces creates sweet harmony in the eating area of this French country kitchen. The armoire and decorative door bear characteristics of different provinces but are unified by their height, while the traditional slat-style garden chairs and a walnut dining table are equally overscale. All the pieces in the room display bold angles and possess the same raw-boned feeling brought on by years of beloved use.*

RIGHT: *Even breakfast takes on a festive mood in a kitchen where the dichotomy between fancy and plain is palpable. The antique table and characteristically mismatched chairs are simple in style and made of the most basic wood. Nonetheless, silver and pressed linen napkins adorn the table, giving the room a slightly dressy air. More favorite platters, pitchers, bowls, and cups are displayed on the shelves above the built-in buffet.*

ABOVE: *Cooking and entertaining are frequent rather than novel events among most French families, which explains why their kitchens are often designed with row upon row of open shelving laden with bowls, platters, casserole dishes, and other culinary necessities. While practical, the contents also make for an attractive display. In this kitchen, where preparations for a party are under way, everything is within arm's reach, including pitchers, canisters, and some wooden spoons, forks, and a rolling pin crammed into an old jar.*

LEFT: *Used as a crucial ingredient in many dishes and imbibed during family and company meals, wine is just as integral a part of the French country kitchen as are appliances, cookware, food, and utensils. In the corner of such a kitchen, far enough from the sources of heat so that the contents are not endangered, sits a simple, painted-blue farmhouse rack that houses the family's stash. The bottles have been lovingly collected through the years and gingerly laid on their sides to age.*

RIGHT: *In this inviting kitchen, ceramic tiles sporting a shade of blue that is reminiscent of the Mediterranean on a sunny day line the backsplash, create an easy-to-clean resting spot for food and utensils, and adorn the hood of the stove. Other characteristically French country elements include a pot rack with heavy copper pots and saucepans, handcrafted wooden cabinetry, a framed fruit print, an old hanging lamp, and a cherished white porcelain stove that has been in the family for decades.*

LEFT: *Kitchens are for relaxing as well as for eating and cooking. In this large multipurpose kitchen, a small recess in the stone wall proved the perfect place for a banquette. Upholstered in a geometric blue-and-white fabric, the piece echoes the collection of faience above. The white metal bread box, a modern twist on the traditional wood panetière carved to store bread, was included more as a whimsical decorative touch than as a practical place for safekeeping fresh baguettes.*

BELOW: *In the spirit of a typical French country kitchen, this space includes a variety of materials, styles, and proportions that combine to create an eclectic whole, causing the room to appear as though it evolved through the years. Moreover, various specific elements of French country styling have been integrated into the cabinetry: the center island manifests deep carving typical of Normandy, and the spindled plate guards on the corner unit are taken from the dressoirs of Brittany. The cabinetry, beams, floorboards, table, chairs, and stools bring in a wide range of woods, while the green marble on the island acts as an elegant contemporary foil.*

OPPOSITE: *Traditional furnishings that would look just as proper in a living room or dining room are used in French country kitchens to add dignity as well as to provide practical services. Here, a long pine buffet with drawers and a bottom shelf adds charm while housing cookbooks. The piece mixes well with a walnut china rack that displays a favorite collection of faience and Chinese-inspired dessert plates and cups. Baskets for plants and bread contribute to the casual ambience, as does the border paper, which boasts a simple cornucopia motif.*

LEFT: *Aside from the pot rack, nothing epitomizes quintessential French style like the baker's rack, which is used for storage and display. Here, a baker's rack made of wrought iron and brass shows off an eclectic collection of objets d'art, plants, and wine in a kitchen that has been handsomely papered in two distinct fabrics sharing the common denominator of a blue-and-white color scheme. Both designs—large checks and a toile de Jouy—are equally representative of French country style and are never passé.*

BELOW: *In this corner of a French country kitchen, French ladder-back armchairs with rush seats are grouped around a plain wood table that has been dressed up with a handsome white linen cloth. A fireplace graced by a wooden mantel, as well as a cloth frill twisted across the opening to give the chimney draw and prevent soot from darkening the wall, offers visual warmth while the fire within provides comfort on cold winter days. A nearby built-in floor-to-ceiling cabinet stores dishes and other items for table settings.*

ABOVE: *An attractive still life with a French country flavor can be fashioned from such simple elements as a big bouquet of fresh flowers placed in front of bottles of oil, vinegar, and flavored liqueurs. And the best part of the arrangement is that it can change frequently, bringing something new to the kitchen on a regular basis.*

RIGHT: *An imposing eighteenth-century walnut vaisselier from Brittany features the province's classic spindled plate guards. With its deep red painted back, the piece provides a dramatic resting spot for a collection of different Limoges china dinner plates. Adding more personality to the scene are a large glass vase of fresh flowers and a generous soup tureen, the latter of which is also from Limoges.*

BELOW: *This ceiling, with its joists supported by and embedded in the tops of the beams, is so characteristic of the French farmhouse that the style is referred to as à la française. Although the rest of the kitchen is not specifically French, the ceiling sets an overwhelmingly French tone. Herbs dangling from old recycled beams at the tops of some of the windows contribute to this feeling, as does the selection of rustic materials, including the brick used to face the cabinet that houses a cooktop and oven.*

ABOVE: *An important part of life in the French countryside has been drying herbs and flowers, a craft that is still being practiced today in this kitchen. Together with collections of kitchen utensils and various odds and ends, the dried herbs and flowers make the space come alive in a crowded yet appealing way. Small wrought-iron skillets, old knives, and other kitchen bric-a-brac adorn the brick wall beside the now purely decorative fireplace, which is currently home to some brass and copper tea kettles. Heavy ceramic jugs, once filled with wine but now only ornamental, rest peacefully on the floor.*

BELOW: *The spirit of this eat-in kitchen resonates with an American country feeling on account of its wooden walls, flooring, and door, along with its simple painted furnishings. However, the space does boast some distinctly French touches, including a large tin pail filled with dried flowers and the mixing of pieces of furniture painted in different hues.*

ABOVE: *An old stone farmhouse kitchen with a restored open timbered ceiling has been modernized for a family that likes to cook, though the room still retains its country feeling. The roof has been opened with skylights; a two-level center island was constructed to offer distinct spaces for cooking and cleaning; and a wooden table and chair have been added to provide another place for labor-intensive cooking chores. Irregularly shaped flagstones line the floor, helping to visually unify the kitchen's many textures, materials, and subtle wood tones.*

RIGHT: *In a small landscaped courtyard off a kitchen, a former butcher's table has been topped by festive blue-and-white tiles, transforming it into a place to enjoy a game of dominoes and some wine on a pleasant afternoon. The Breton blue color scheme is carried through in the painted chair (brought outdoors from the kitchen) and lovely cut crystal goblets that seem almost too good to be used outdoors.*

RIGHT: *Touches of French country styling permeate this kitchen, which has a decidedly dressy instead of typically casual demeanor. The Provençal-inspired tablecloth has been deepened for a richer look; the white country lace curtains have been gussied up with shirring; and the traditional pot rack has been relegated to an out-of-the-way alcove.*

BELOW: *In this quaint kitchen, pale pine faces all the cabinetry, which is enhanced by both delicately patterned and solid blues. Square blue-and-white tiles in two patterns line the backsplash, echoing the collection of plates that accent the area above the windows. Further splashes of blue include the painted window casements and chairs. Even the hand towel boasts a blue-and-white Provençal design.*

ABOVE: *As in many French kitchens, the china—or at least a large portion of it—is perpetually on display. The almost all white background of this room adds a crisp freshness and timeless appeal, also typical of Scandinavian design.*

LEFT: *Rows of hardworking copper cookware and a long trestle table make this French country kitchen appropriate for a large family that entertains frequently. But it is the beamed ceiling that gives the space its authenticity. Other rustic elements, such as the fireplace and the stone floor, inspired the owners to refrain from painting over the wall's rough stucco finish. Adjacent to the double range is an old stone country sink, which is useful for filling pots.*

RIGHT, TOP: *A limestone-and-tile sink, decked in traditional blue and white, was the inspiration for the striking blue shade of paint used on these walls. A built-in wall cupboard, set off from the rest of the room with a deeper hue, provides space-efficient storage in the small kitchen, which receives natural light from a small dormer window.*

RIGHT, BOTTOM: *A fancy Louis XVI–style armchair brings an elegant touch to the casual blue-and-white cotton skirted table at one end of a small kitchen. The painted blue window frame adds more color and eliminates the need for curtains so that the lush landscape outdoors is always in view.*

ABOVE: *The old-style French kitchen frequently becomes a beehive of activity, as evidenced by this room. Atop the tiled counter, fresh greenery is readied for use in a centerpiece; a lower counter is covered with fresh vegetables that will be made into a salad; and the ledge above the stove is crammed end-to-end with jars of preserves and pickled vegetables. Copper cookware decorates the walls, while blue-and-white pottery and tiles provide refreshing color. The recycled wooden gate, a charming reminder of the home's farmhouse origins, leads into the living room beyond.*

RIGHT: *The eating area in this French country cottage kitchen demonstrates the wonders of the simpler things in life. A bouquet of colorful garden flowers in an old tub, a rustic wooden plank table that coordinates beautifully with the kitchen walls, and fetching painted-blue chairs that add a welcome splash of color create a wonderful spot for a tête-à-tête that is just as appealing as a much grander setting. An assortment of old stainless steel utensils hanging on the wall brings additional panache to the setup.*

BELOW: *Large cast-iron cookers, now defunct, anchor this simply furnished room, the windows of which were deliberately left uncurtained to contribute to the no-nonsense ambience. Above the cooking area, an assortment of tiles is configured to resemble a piece of artwork. These tiles, along with similar ones lining the dado and big copper pots and earthenware casually arranged on shelves and against walls, are the prime sources of color in the decor. Simple ladder-back chairs and an absolutely plain rectangular wooden table occupy the center of the space, creating a good work surface as well as a fine place to dine.*

BELOW: *Tall topiary bushes stand guard at the end of a dining table in a kitchen that is classically French and casually chic with its stone arch, overhead beams, and pine table and ladder-back chairs. Distinguishing the host from the rest of the diners, a tapestry-covered wing chair is positioned at the head of the table, where it adds an air of importance. A simple armoire with a nonetheless commanding presence stands tall and proud nearby, making dining essentials easily accessible.*

BELOW: *With a typically French sleight of hand, a decrepit old clock in the room shown at left is transformed into an attention grabber. Framed with a hand-painted border and topped with a slew of dried roses, it becomes an architectural element rather than a mere antique.*

ABOVE: *In this elegant château, the kitchen was designed to look like and function as a space meant more for romantic old-world entertaining than cooking. Nevertheless, all the necessary appliances are present, though a bit camouflaged by wonderful old materials and paint finishes. The walls of the room were frescoed and painted to resemble wood paneling, with the insets a subtle blue-gray, ringed by the palest taupe and an antique gold. Blending in harmoniously with the color scheme, terra-cotta tiles line the floor and mirror the color of the painted ceiling. Even the accessories reflect old-world styling, including a painted Louis XV chair, an elegant damask tablecloth, and dried flowers turned upside down to fill a former hood.*

ROOMS FOR RETREAT

Bedrooms, at least as we now know them, were rarely found before the nineteenth century in the French countryside, where the habit of sleeping by the fire in the *salle* was widespread. Any bedrooms that did exist were used to house the girls of a family, and such spaces were sparsely furnished with merely a bed or two and a simple wardrobe.

Loft-style sleeping alcoves under the rafters were more common for those not sleeping by the fire. Eventually, many of these were adapted to become entire rooms. This evolution led to the quintessential French country bedroom tucked away under the pitched beamed ceilings of a provincial cottage.

Since the bedroom (if a household was wealthy enough to have one) was a communal space, provincial beds were constructed so as to provide privacy as well as warmth. Many were draped with hangings so the occupants could dress without being seen. These textiles also performed the helpful duties of keeping out dust, dirt, bugs, and cold air.

As the wealth of a household increased, so too did the beauty of its beds. Most were at least four feet (122cm) wide, designed to accommodate two occupants. The beds had thick mattresses made of straw or, in wealthier homes, feathers, and they were topped with large feather quilts and homemade sheets and blankets. Because they were usually placed against a wall or in an alcove, they were heavily carved on one side and plainly finished on the other.

Different types of beds became popular in different regions of France. High box beds (*lits-clos*), totally enclosed by wooden panels that were often richly carved and colorfully painted, were prominent in Brittany, Normandy, Auvergne, and parts of the Alps. (In the Alps, sheep slept underneath them, serving as bedwarmers.)

Beds with canopies attached to the bedposts or suspended from the ceilings, running the gamut from full overhangs to half-testers, prevailed throughout all the provinces but reflected regional differences. Angel beds (*lits d'ange*) with four short posts, a plain headboard, no footboard, and half-testers were commonplace in the South, as were *litoches* (the same bed sans the hangings). Elegantly draped beds with full canopies totally concealing the mattress were referred to as *à la duchesse* and could often be found in the North, where the colder climate dictated a more enclosed space.

OPPOSITE: *Despite the fact that these furnishings are pure Louis XV, they look right at home in this French country residence. Though once formal and grand, they now radiate a faded glory that comes from years, perhaps generations, of use. The aura of warmth and comfort is further evoked by the slightly decayed trompe l'oeil paint finishes on the headboard and nightstand and the faded Aubusson-inspired fabrics.*

Creating a French country bedroom today is often as simple as outfitting a room with an ornate bed topped with a canopy of some configuration or a simple bed covered with a traditional provincial textile, such as a *boutis* (an intricately quilted, brightly colored coverlet of Provençal design) or a hand-worked white lace spread. Add a wardrobe, be it simple or elaborate, a coffer, and perhaps a few comfortable country chairs, and *voilà*—the French country bedroom is reborn.

BELOW: *Heavy snow white linens alter the look of this bedroom in a French country home. The dark* lit en bateau *goes from simple to stunning thanks to the pristine spread, while curtains transform the area around the bed into an intimate alcove. A delicate row of lace trim on the bottom of the drapes along with satin cording and tassels keep the textiles from seeming too austere. Meanwhile, a subtle Provençal-style flower pattern on the walls imbues the room with just a hint of color.*

LEFT: *A dark, masculine Empire-style bed becomes airy and romantic with the right trappings in this French country room. By suspending gauzy white cotton from the ceiling, the bed is transformed into an alluring* lit en baldaquin *(canopy bed). The blue-and-white color scheme gives the room its lively spirit and makes the space seem as though it has been patterned after a set of Chinese-inspired faience from a French village.*

BELOW: *A picture is worth a thousand words, and the stunning* toile de Jouy *that envelops this bedroom radiates the message that this is a stately French room. The traditional fabric originated in Jouy in the mid-eighteenth century and is well known for its large pictorial repeats appearing in a single bold color. The grand aura that such a pattern usually imparts is toned down a bit here with a white linen coverlet and a white ladder-back chair.*

ABOVE: *An eclectic mix of elements adds up to definitive French country style in this attic bedroom. Its charm comes from a blend of fine period pieces of disparate pedigrees, including an Art Nouveau brass bed and an Empire chest, as well as the subtle contrasting color scheme of white and pale gray. The deep earthy hues of the furnishings, which include not only the bed and chest but also a stack of rattan storage cases and an old wooden chair, serve as the unifying element.*

OPPOSITE: *Lace textiles were de rigueur in fashionable European homes during the eighteenth and nineteenth centuries, and were made into curtains, coverlets, and tablecloths. They were particularly adored in the French countryside, almost as much as the hand-blocked floral fabrics of Provence. In this bedroom, a provincial lace coverlet gives the space its French country ambience, though the other furnishings—an Art Nouveau wrought-iron bed and basket and a painted rush-seat chair—are also authentic French country pieces.*

ABOVE: *Box beds, which were enclosed on three sides and shuttered or draped on their fourth edge, were popular in the French countryside for their privacy and capacity to keep out drafts. Outfitted with huge straw mattresses and large feather-filled duvets, they were beautifully carved and sometimes sported painted finishes like the one shown here. Today, they are more romantic than pragmatic, possessing the ability to infuse a contemporary room with a country tone.*

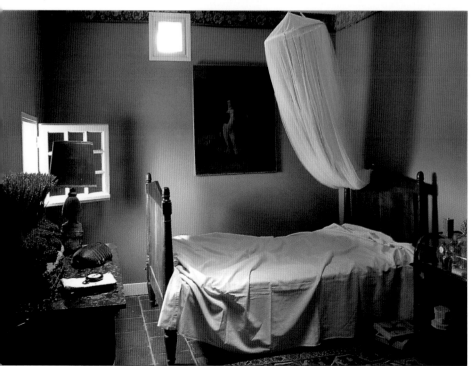

Since clay was abundant in some of the southern French provinces, many homes in those areas had tile floors. These surfaces offered the benefits of being cool in the summer, warm in the winter, and easy to clean year-round. Here, two Provence-inspired bedrooms have such floors, as well as small windows and mosquito netting to keep the heat and bugs at bay. The creative use of some other trappings typical of Provençal interiors, including a border inspired by the fabrics of the region (LEFT) and a traditional boutis (ABOVE), effortlessly imbues these rooms with the flavor of the French countryside.

LEFT: *Often, all it takes is one strong element to bestow a certain style upon a room. The bed in this simply furnished room could be from Sweden or Belgium, and the cream-colored linens with lace edging are ubiquitous throughout Europe. But the charming chair, with its regal gilt finish and an endearing fleur-de-lis emblazoned on its medallion back, is unmistakably Louis XV, thereby giving this otherwise generic country look a French flavor.*

LEFT: *Instead of the furnishings, it is the fabrics and decorative moldings that give this room its romantic country appeal. The exuberant French chintz is used as a duvet and repeated on part of the back wall to simulate a headboard. Cream accents in the molding and pure white linens soften the loftiness of the setting, making it far less formal.*

ABOVE: *Set in an alcove topped with an ornate cornice, a Louis XVI daybed is effectively separated from the rest of the room. Matching fauteuils that face the hearth make it clear that the space does double duty as a sitting room. The two areas are unified by two small Oriental rugs bearing similar hues and by the dramatic shade of red used on the daybed and the chairs' upholstery.*

BELOW: *With the help of a bed crown, a traditional* lit d'ange *has been recreated in this room. But instead of being draped in opulent tapestries, the bed is graced by a rustic chintz that gives the room its country flavor. Other modest textiles used in unusual ways include a gauzy cotton backdrop for the vanity and translucent window curtains caught with tiebacks and puddled to perfection on the floor.*

ABOVE: *The ambience projected by a simple window dressed in white and accented with a few well-chosen accessories can be sufficient for certain rooms when a spare, rather than overdone or crowded, look is desired. A humble French lace hankie may have served as raw material for these country curtains, but the overall effect of the tableau, which exudes charisma, is anything but plain.*

RIGHT: *This nineteenth-century wrought-iron daybed could be of any origin, but it takes on a distinctly French persona in these surroundings thanks to creamy lace-trimmed linens and the magnificent French windows that lie beyond. Draping these windows with layers of simple billowing cotton instead of something more ornate also contributes to the effect and keeps the tone of the space on track.*

ABOVE: *Outfitted with aged, but not vintage, fixtures, this predominantly white bathroom, or* salle de bain, *is bathed in country appeal thanks to a winsome bucolic mural. Even such refined French antiques as a crystal chandelier, a Louis XVI–style stool, gilt-framed prints, and fancy sconces cannot deprive the space of its rustic grandeur.*

LEFT: *Here, decorative devices derived from French country styling spruce up what otherwise would be considered a fairly plain washroom. A Provençal-inspired floral cotton was used for the balloon shades, the skirt of an old porcelain sink, the liner of the clothing hamper, and the trim of the fauteuil. Note the crisp white lattice work, which masks a thoroughly routine tub, making the cleansing experience in this space somewhat akin to bathing outdoors.*

BELOW: *The vernacular of this Normandy cottage, with its timber detailing and chalky walls, shows up even in the washroom, which was probably a bed chamber when the home was originally built. Because of the strong architectural elements of the room, the furnishings become less important. At the same time, though, certain pieces stand out, including a primitive milking stool, a wicker armchair softened with a large cushion, and a dressy Oriental carpet, all of which assume a country demeanor thanks to the surroundings.*

Part Two

ITALIAN
COUNTRY

INTRODUCTION

Piu se spenne e pejo se magna. A curious expression, although one heard frequently in homes, markets, and local trattorias throughout the Italian countryside. Literally the proverb says, "The more one pays, the worse one eats," although the spirit of the words is lost in translation. In Italy, where hours are often spent luxuriating *a tavola*, or at the table, culinary rhapsody often inspires proverbial wisdom. The food that nourishes these ideas is remarkably uncomplicated, made from fresh, natural ingredients prepared in a simple way. What could be more delicious or easier to make than *un sugo di pomodoro*, a pasta sauce made with olive oil, garlic, ripe tomatoes, and a few sprigs of fresh basil? Italian country life is just as sweet and simple. The proverb, in fact, celebrates this lifestyle as much as it warns against the pitfalls of more indulgent cuisine. Long and languorous afternoons spent dining alfresco—in the dappled shade of a pergola overlooking the Italian countryside, perhaps—aptly demonstrate the wisdom of the words.

The Italian *campagna*, or countryside, stretches the length of the peninsula, from the northern Alps to the southern coasts of the Mediterranean, but it is the natural beauty of the central peninsula that conjures the most vivid images of Italian country life. The landscape, rustic architecture, and simple lifestyle of this region have come to define true Italian country living for most Italians and Italophiles alike.

The landscape of central Italy is marked by gentle umber hills and majestic cypresses feathering the sky. Roads twist along sheep pastures and broad meadows, and olive trees shimmer in the sun. One cannot fail to notice the quality and variety of light as the sun moves across the sky, continually altering the palette of this rugged terrain.

Nestled along peaks and valleys, far removed from roadways, sit quaint farmhouses—*case coloniche*—which appear as natural in this landscape as the vineyards and copper fields over which they preside. These farmhouses are typically built like small fortresses. Walls are constructed of creamy beige stone and roofs are covered with *coppi*, curved terra-cotta tiles. From the outside these houses appear squat and strong, classically proportioned. They are large but self-contained and rarely have more than two floors.

OPPOSITE: *Vineyards abound throughout Tuscany. During the* vendemmia, *or grape harvest, friends, family, and neighbors pick grapes at a feverish pace while the fruit is perfectly ripe. Three years later, the wine is ready for toasting.*

These farmsteads are simple and unpretentious, having originally been the exclusive domain of *contadini*, the tenant farmers who worked the land under the *mezzadria* sharecropping system. After the system was abolished in the 1950s, farm laborers left the country to seek better wages in the cities. In many cases, farmhouses that had been in families for generations were abandoned. In recent decades, as the modern world has become increasingly hectic, a new appreciation has emerged for these dilapidated old farmhouses, which are bought and converted into splendid country retreats. Medieval towers and small castles, relics from the age of warring city-states, as well as abbeys, monasteries, and grand villas are also real estate prime for renovation. It is the simple farmhouse, however, so elegant in its design and modest in its means, that embodies the essence of Italian country life.

For visitors from all over the world, the charm of the Italian countryside has proved irresistible. The British were the first to arrive, buying up properties in Tuscany early in the twentieth century. The Italians themselves were slow to follow and only in recent years began buying country houses in large numbers.

Converting farmhouses is not as simple as throwing on a few coats of paint. Often farmsteads are not equipped with running water or proper sanitation. Electrical wiring can be scary at best. Farm tenants lived in quarters upstairs, which were reached by external wooden staircases. Quite a bit of remodeling is often necessary as well, because the ground floors of most *case coloniche* were originally constructed as animal stables. The ground floor is commonly converted into a kitchen and living area, and the vaulted brick ceilings are, in some instances, painted white. Internal staircases must be added, and

if the house is to be used during the winter, a heating system will likely have to be installed. All in all, renovating is no small task. Nevertheless, city dwellers still flock to the country undeterred.

Renovated interiors are spacious and comfortable. Furnishings are few and include only finely made, modestly designed pieces. To maintain a sense of rustic authenticity, rooms remain largely undecorated. Walls and floors are left bare, ceiling beams exposed. The spare symmetry of the decor and the simplicity of the furnishings emphasize the strength and boldness of the architecture. The natural elements come together in a concert of texture and color. Smooth surfaces play against rough, warm tones against cool.

The austere design of Italian country houses reflects the ruggedness of the surrounding landscape. It is this earthbound quality that makes life in the Italian countryside so enchanting. In every aspect, country retreats suggest a life far removed from the stress and strain of the modern world. The rustic nature of *le case coloniche*—like the uncomplicated goodness of the local cuisine—characterizes a refreshing way of life, one that embraces simple pleasures and is in many ways uniquely Italian. *La dolce vita* indeed.

OPPOSITE: *This living room's tall, vaulted brick ceiling serves as a reminder that the space once functioned as an animal stall. The room is now spacious and elegant, with a chair and sofa covered in simple white cotton, a time-honored country standard. The floors have an earthy, matte finish that visually softens the decor. Hanging baskets filled with dried herbs and flowers are a nice rustic touch.*

LEFT: *Hanging from ceiling beams or displayed on countertops, cooking utensils can bring fascinating geometry to the kitchen. A good heavy mortar and pestle is a wonderfully simple implement—a remarkable synthesis of form and function. A hanging bread stand is perhaps more whimsical, but nevertheless interesting to look at. Wooden spoons and ladles are usually kept in jars beside the stove to ensure easy access during frequent cooking frenzies.*

RIGHT: *In this Italian country-style bedroom, little can be done to enhance the majestic vaulted octagon ceiling. Such a setting requires only bare white walls and a polished wood floor to make it a place of beauty.*

ARCHITECTURAL DETAILS

The beauty of *la casa colonica* lies in the integrity of its building materials and the solidity of its construction. The Italian farmhouse is very much a sum of its parts, and in most cases the parts haven't changed for generations. From the *colombaia*, or dovecote, at the crown of the roof to the rosy *cotto* floor, the country house appears almost the same today as it did a century ago. That, of course, is the lure of the Italian countryside. The sense of timelessness is what fascinates.

Building materials are as old as the land itself and, in many cases, pulled right from the earth. Wood and stone form the foundation of all country houses, and even manmade elements such as stucco and terra-cotta, which translates literally as "cooked earth," reflect their natural origins. The combination of these materials, with their warm colors and rich textures, gives *la casa colonica* its rustic elegance.

The walls of Italian farmhouses are fortress-thick, sometimes more than two feet (46cm) wide to protect against heat and cold. They are built with local stones that are joined with lime mortar. Inside walls are generally left bare or are covered with a coarse, rich layer of stucco. Stone walls can also be painted with pink- or sepia-toned earth dyes, which lend the stones and mortar a mellow glow. In any case, the texture of the walls suggests the integrity of their construction. Nothing is hidden here, and the simplicity of form and function is refreshing. Not surprisingly, very few paintings hang on the walls. If a painting is put up, it usually commands an entire wall.

The rough texture of the walls plays well against the smooth surfaces of the terra-cotta floors. Red *cotto* bricks and tiles are often used to cover every floor in the house, although hardwood floors are not uncommon. Terra-cotta tiles are usually rectangular, a shape well-suited for intricate herringbone designs. Generally the floors are polished and waxed to a high gloss, although a weathered, matte finish can be effective as well. The older the tiles get, the more serene and impressionistic they become. Time and traffic smooth the tiles and give them a soft quality. Rooms are never carpeted wall-to-wall, although oriental rugs, kilims, or sisal rugs are occasionally used to accentuate the warm hues of the terra-cotta.

OPPOSITE: *Solid masonry is the foundation of every Italian countryside villa or farmhouse. Shutters help insulate the house from intense summer heat. Curved terra-cotta tiles known as* coppi *cover roofs and entryways. Nature is an integral design component: ivy slithers up walls, while wisteria creeps along the pergola and the second-floor loggia.*

Massive and splendid wooden beams support the ceilings of most farmhouses. Hand-sawn and roughly striated, these beams are usually made of oak or chestnut and given a glossy coat of wax. On these large beams rest smaller, perpendicular wooden joists, which in turn support thin bricks called *pianelle*, the base for the floor tiles above. This complex network of beams and joists creates a visually interesting space. Leaving these heavy beams exposed brings a sense of musculature to the room. In some rooms—bedrooms especially—the ceilings are whitewashed to lessen their severity and create a more intimate setting.

To aid in insulating the house, windows are traditionally small and deep-set, adding to the building's staunch disposition. Inside and out, louvered shutters are used to protect against the beating sun. Curtains were not traditionally hung, although in recent times sheer, elegant drapes have been employed to soften the effect of bare windows. With or without curtains, the shutters remain. Outside they are stained dark brown or painted in verdant or ocher hues; inside they are commonly painted white.

In keeping with the castlelike construction of the house, external doors are often quite imposing. Doorways, like windows, are distinguished by travertine or *pietra serena* lintels set in the walls. Heavy wooden front doors are decorated with bolts, hinges, and other ironmongery that would have traditionally been made by the local blacksmith. In renovated farmhouses, more delicate French doors have been installed in the archways where cowshed doors once hung, opening onto sprawling terraces.

ABOVE: *Fine craftsmanship is the hallmark of Italian country design. These graceful French doors lead from living room to terrace in a renovated farmhouse. Ironically, animals once passed through this archway as they came and went from their stalls. The farmhouse conversion was impeccable, however, and the result is a typically simple, elegant Italian domain.*

RIGHT: *Although running water is now enjoyed throughout Italy, a private well was considered a luxury not so long ago. This renovated seventeenth-century villa has kept its carved marble font as a picturesque memento of the past. The wrought-iron wellhead, window grates, and carved masonry attest to the skill of generations of local craftsmen.*

LEFT: *Ruddy salmon is perhaps the color most emblematic of Italian dwellings. Warm and subtle, this reddish-orange hue changes with the passage of the day and is deliciously evocative of the scorching Mediterranean sun. This ubiquitous tint actually looks better with age and seems to take on an entirely new countenance over the years. Here, tendrils of dark green ivy climb the walls, creating a vivid contrast of hot and cold colors.*

RIGHT: *Reflecting the influence of countless Mediterranean cultures over the centuries, Italy's southern landscape features some of the country's most unique architecture. Hundreds of years old, the domed houses of Alberobello are a perfect example. To insulate against the scorching heat, walls are several feet thick and vaulted roofs are stacked high with terra-cotta bricks.*

BELOW: *A bird's-eye view of a hillside town reveals an intricate patchwork of tiled rooftops resembling a cubist collage. Curved terra-cotta roof tiles are prevalent throughout tne Mediterranean, yet each region has a distinctive hue. Terra cotta is—simply translated—cooked earth, so the color and texture of the local soil are directly reflected in the architecture.*

ABOVE: *Villa architecture is simple and elegant, marked by low-arched tile roofs with wide eaves and either stone or stucco walls. Decoration is spare but refined, limited to molded lintels above doors and windows and slender, wrought-iron balustrades along balconies.*

LEFT: *In northern Italy, the influence of Gothic architecture is apparent in many of the older country villas. The carved stone balcony of this former monastery opens onto a courtyard. Doors and windows are accented with both trefoil and pointed lancet arches, as well as decorative spiral columns. Picturesque decay enhances the exterior walls, where layers of stucco have deteriorated to reveal the original red brick.*

ABOVE: *Roadside trattorias and taverns in the countryside are rather inconspicuous, sometimes marked by little more than a small painted sign. The decor is typically quite spare, although a bombastic wrought-iron* gallo, *or rooster, typifies the lighthearted spirit of many country artisans.*

RIGHT: *The forest regions to the north feature some of the most intriguing architecture in the Italian countryside. Here, a nineteenth-century house literally merges with nature. Ivy climbing the walls lends an aspect of fantasy and evokes a mysterious charm.*

ABOVE: *This renovated* casa colonica *is a paragon of Italian country style. All the building materials reflect the colors and textures of the surrounding landscape, from the* pietra serena *stone walls to the terra-cotta* colombaia, *or dovecote, on the roof. The design of the house is modest yet well proportioned, a study in simple elegance.*

RIGHT: *Modern country houses adhere to the same aesthetic principles of more antiquated retreats. Here, the interplay of contrasting colors and textures is remarkable. Salmon-colored stucco walls are infused with strands of lush green ivy. Black shutters accent white windows and intensify the rich verdant hues of the lawn and vine-covered pergola. Even the terra-cotta planters in the garden complement the* coppi *roof tiles.*

LEFT: *Along the Amalfi Coast, buildings are often whitewashed inside and out. This pergola has classical plaster columns and a bamboo trellis roof. Pristine white curtains further protect the terrace from the sweltering sun and look quite elegant as well. Blue seat cushions give off a cool glow.*

RIGHT: *On the island of Capri, many terraces are white-washed and trimmed with glazed ceramic tiles. Often these handmade tiles tell a story—historical or legendary—that relates to the island. Here, the tile work—an artist's vision of what the harbor may have looked like a century or so ago—seems to mirror the scene below it.*

ABOVE: *Here, an oasis of lush foliage seems to transform the piazza into a tranquil country getaway. The small towns dotting the Italian countryside do, in fact, feel quite removed from the pressures of the modern world, and offer great weekend escapes from life in the city.*

LEFT: *Statuary is found not only on manicured estates, but also in the more modest gardens of the average casa colonica. A phalanx of Renaissance statues lends an air of antiquity to a grove of potted lemon trees in this charming garden.*

BELOW: *Typically overgrown by ivy, statues nestled in shrubbery or otherwise absorbed by nature imbue outdoor spaces with a sense of antiquity. Stone putti, or cherubs, enliven many Italian gardens.*

OPPOSITE, TOP: *Sheltered within the medieval town walls of Lucca, the sprawling Villa Torreggiani features a host of classical garden follies and statuary. The impressive staircase leads from a radiant flower garden to a broad, majestic fountain lined with sculptures.*

BELOW: *Italy boasts some of the world's most opulent country estates, and Villa Maser is certainly one of the grandest of all. In the gardens, a baroque, nineteenth-century temple folly is decorated with a pantheon of reveling Dionysian nymphs and cherubs.*

ABOVE: *Located on the slopes of the Dolomites, this rustic chalet is indicative of many houses in the region. Small windows help insulate against cold in the winter, while high-pitched gables keep snow from piling up on the roof. Similarly, long eaves protect the entrances and walkways from heavy snowfalls. Rough-hewn wood beams and walls made from local blond stone integrate the house into its natural surrounding.*

ABOVE: *The canals of Treviso wind along lovely homes as well as several charming old factories. This brick textile mill dates from the early twentieth century. With eaves rising and falling and colorful bands of paint lining the walls, the building itself makes an interesting weave.*

KITCHENS AND DINING ROOMS

For all of its worldly treasures, Italy is perhaps most renowned for its exquisite and simple cuisine. The land that spawned Etruscan civilization, the Roman Empire, and the Renaissance is celebrated just as roundly for *gnocchi di patate*, *ravioli verdi*, and *risotto coi funghi*. It should come as no surprise, then, that the kitchen—the font of these delicacies—is the heart and soul of the Italian household. In the countryside especially, where the pace of the day allows a more subtle appreciation for good food and talk, life revolves around mealtimes and the kitchen and dining room.

Because of the closeness of the Italian family, mealtime is sacred in many households even today. From the morning's espresso to *la pranza*, or lunch, at midday and finally *la cena*, or dinner, families still choose to eat together at the kitchen table whenever possible. And more often than not, meals are taken in leisure, the food and company well savored.

The design of the Italian country kitchen is as simple and timeless as the meals prepared there. White plaster walls, terra-cotta tile floor, exposed beam ceiling—these elements are the foundation of the traditional *cucina rustica*. Like all Italian interiors, the kitchen is kept *ben sistemato*—organized and neat. Surfaces are uncluttered and the overall aspect of the room is spare and minimal.

Although renovated country houses are well accessorized with the latest stovetops and ovens, the massive, smoke-stained hearth or brick oven still conjures images of the Italian mother tending black cauldrons of boiling pasta hanging over the fire. The sink was traditionally made of hand-hewn travertine marble or *pietra serena*, a provincial stone, although more modern enamel sinks are certainly suitable. Local ceramic tiles are often set around the sink area and on countertops, usually in bright, vivid colors that look wonderful against the kitchen's backdrop of earth tones. Wooden cupboards are usually built into the walls to hold dishes and pantry goods.

La tavola, or the table, is one of the most essential pieces of furniture in the Italian home. Nothing else epitomizes country living quite like the kitchen table. Italians can spend hours around the table, enjoying a meal with friends and relatives, telling stories, and laughing, above all. The table

OPPOSITE: *In Italy, country charm is all in the details: a wreath of pinecones on the wall and a miniature greenhouse of herbs and spices beside a stoneware* acqua *pitcher on the windowsill. Bentwood chairs and hand-painted wall tiles complete the setting.*

is typically long and rectangular, made of heavy, coarse pine or chestnut. The top is well-worn and smooth, with nicks and scratches only adding to its charm. Chairs are simple in design, with slightly frayed rush seats giving a lived-in look.

Another traditional kitchen furnishing is the *madia*, a small cabinet table that once served as a bread cupboard. Today it is typically used as portable counter space, as useful for holding a microwave oven as it is for storing bread. A painted wood credenza can be used to display collections of local arts and crafts. The artisan tradition is still very much alive in the Italian countryside, with regional specialties ranging from majolica and pewter to glassware and pottery. A carved wood cassone, or chest can be used to store linens.

Hanging on walls or over the hearth, gleaming copper pots and pans bring unusual geometry and warm color to the kitchen environment. In keeping with the rigorous sense of organization, other cooking implements are readily available at arm's reach. What really makes the Italian country kitchen transcendent is the abundance of fresh produce, especially in the summer months. Rosemary and basil plants growing in terra-cotta pots and hanging baskets or wooden bowls filled with fruits and vegetables give a sense of bounteous country living.

In the dining room, setting the table is an art form in itself. Again, simple elegance is the key, even for casual dining. A crisp white tablecloth is the foundation of the well-dressed table. Italy is renowned for its sumptuous linens which are impeccably woven and embroidered with only the most subtle of patterns and motifs.

Place settings are refined yet understated. Simple white porcelain is appropriate for just about any occasion, but hand-painted ceramics lend a country flavor to more informal affairs. Clear crystal stemware and un-adorned flatware are country standards. A carafe is used for both wine and water for all but the most casual meals, when the bottles can be placed on the table.

ABOVE: *Incredibly, this brilliantly renovated kitchen once served as a cowshed. The conversion left the room wide-open, maximizing the vast sense of space provided by the vaulted ceilings. Uncluttered, smooth surfaces are an Italian trademark—especially in the kitchen, where one finds* tutto a posto, *everything in order.*

ABOVE: *The best dining rooms are comfortable as well as attractive. As many hours are passed at the dining room table, all the senses should be satisfied. Mellow lighting and thin, diaphanous curtains create a cozy and warm ambience. For those fortunate enough to possess a green thumb, an indoor trellis or a few strands of well-trained ivy certainly imbue a rustic quality.*

OPPOSITE: *Floral motifs go a long way in a country decor. Here, small delicate roses decorate the china, which harmonizes perfectly with both the curtains and the glazed wall sconces—splendid bouquets of spring flowers. As a final touch, fresh flowers adorn the table.*

OPPOSITE: *In northern Alpine regions, interiors are commonly paneled in wood. From floor to ceiling, every square inch of this kitchen seems to be covered in lovely blond pine. The room's warm, supple glow is augmented by shiny copper pots and pans hanging on the walls.*

RIGHT: *Italian kitchens cannot be outdone for their economy of space. This renovated kitchen benefits from a high ceiling that allows a sleek row of shelves to display peculiar cooking implements. The striated wood floor and cabinets bring unusual texture to the room.*

ABOVE: *Flowing folds of gauze make wonderful drapery in a sunroom. The quality of light is enhanced, and the room takes on an ethereal quality. A wisteria-covered, trompe l'oeil trellis around the entrance blends nicely with real ivy creeping up the walls. In a room so minimally decorated, each detail assumes heightened significance: the table setting is impeccable and the terra-cotta-tiled floor exudes a warm glow.*

OPPOSITE: *This dining room has an unmistakably English flavor. The blue and white checked tablecloth and upholstery make dining indoors feel rather like a picnic. That, of course, is the idea of a country retreat. The china and glassware impeccably complement the color theme.*

RIGHT: *Lighting plays an important role in every interior. Here, especially, the lighting has a vital effect on the ambience. The wall sconces radiate a soft light that captures the subtle nuances of the lime-painted walls. Too much light would wash out the color entirely. As it is, the room has a warm, intimate glow.*

BELOW: *Rural decors can be quite modern without sacrificing the simplicity of country living. Although the furniture in this dining area is contemporary in design, it is similar to more traditional country pieces in its heavy, spare construction and minimal decoration.*

ABOVE: *The generous proportions and unusual architecture of many farmhouses allow for quite extraordinary conversions. The ground floor—commonly animal stables in traditional case coloniche—is where contemporary renovators give their imaginations free reign. Vaulted ceilings often provide a majestic dining room setting. Large barn doors are usually replaced by delicate windows or French doors leading to a terrace garden.*

ABOVE: *Original architectural details bring a sense of history to many renovated country retreats. Here, a massive, nineteenth-century olive press occupies the corner of a dining room, remembering the days when the farm produced olive oil. Such an unusual piece of machinery makes the room truly unique. Of course, the other furnishings are remarkable as well—particularly the beautiful Persian rugs, antique leather chairs, and marble table.*

OPPOSITE: *Even in modern country decors, the integrity and nobleness of building materials are apparent. Walls are covered in thick plaster and given a subtle lime wash of color. Balustrades and window grilles are cast in sturdy wrought iron, and delicate French doors open onto a brick terrace.*

RIGHT, TOP: *A glass-enclosed breakfast room is a perfect addition to a country retreat. Life in the countryside is all about communing with nature, and what better way than to take the morning's espresso surrounded by lush greenery.*

RIGHT, BOTTOM: *Nothing symbolizes Italian country living quite like the kitchen table. It is here where family and friends convene several times a day to enjoy each other's company over a good meal. The table is generally made of heavy, knotted, thick-cut wood. The smooth, polished surface shows the hieroglyphic stains and scratches of countless gatherings.*

LEFT: *Often hundreds of years old and typically made of carved marble or stone, a splendid old fireplace is the focus of many country dining rooms. In northern regions, ornate wood mantelpieces are also quite common. This rather formal eighteenth-century mantel is well appointed, topped by an antique mirror and flanked by baroque wall sconces.*

OPPOSITE: *Since the dawn of the Renaissance, trompe l'oeil decorative techniques have been employed in homes throughout the Italian countryside. Classical architectural motifs such as columns, pilasters, cornices, and pediments are commonly featured. Ornate wainscoting and floral boughs embellish the walls of this dining room, giving the space architectural definition. The room's classical furnishings enhance the illusion of being in an ancient Roman salon.*

RIGHT: *Some of the most beautiful aspects of Italian country architecture can be appreciated only from the inside. Massive roof supports line the ceiling of this second-floor kitchen, giving the room an interesting linear configuration. A skylight provides warm lighting and opens up the space.*

BELOW: *Even informal table settings feel special in the cozy confines of an Italian kitchen. Red and white gingham fabric is a country standard, and a deeply polished table certainly enhances the dining experience.*

OPPOSITE: *The flavor of Italian country living comes through in this rustic dining room with its exposed wood beam ceilings, walls lined with fine wines, linen tablecloth, and decorative place settings.*

LEFT: *This Alpine kitchen impresses with its rustic simplicity and rich textures. The architecture is remarkably sturdy, fortified with dark hardwood floors, heavy ceiling beams, and walls covered with coarse plaster. The massive, rough-hewn furniture complements the room perfectly. Although modern conveniences like a stove and radiator have been added, the original oven remains, its doors painted an enchanting red.*

ABOVE: *Rustic indeed, this dining room seems like a hollow in the earth's crust. The bare stone walls have a cavernous quality that is nevertheless made to feel quite cozy. The wall sconces have a chiaroscuro effect on the rough surfaces and cast a warm glow across the deeply polished ceiling. A finely embroidered white tablecloth brightens the setting as well. Slender, wrought-iron chairs complete the scene.*

OPPOSITE: *A pantry off the kitchen can be used to store produce and is often quite picturesque in its own right. A bounty of fresh fruits and vegetables hanging from the rafters or filling a marble basin captures the essence of country living. The rough-hewn modesty of the pantry is perhaps its most poignant quality.*

LIVING SPACES

Italians are a loquacious people. They enjoy good, spirited conversation. A lazy country afternoon is occasion enough to celebrate with hours of laughing and talking. In cool months these hours are passed *nel salotto*, in the living room, but whenever possible Italians like to be outside on a terrace or under a portico.

Inside and out, living spaces are remarkable for their simple elegance. In the *salotto* furniture is generally placed around the edge of the room. This arrangement creates a feeling of space and order, but can also imbue a rather formal air. However formal the living room may appear, it is certainly never fussy or stiff. A few well-chosen pieces of furniture, often rough-hewn and heavyset, are positioned to bring out the beauty of the architectural elements. The living room, which is often a converted cowshed, may have a vaulted brick ceiling that gives the room a lofty and especially grand appearance. A rosy terra-cotta floor and softly hued stucco walls lend great warmth and texture to the room. The mantel over the fireplace, while ornately carved, displays only a single vase of flowers or a few collected objects. French doors leading out to the terrace garden are graceful, the windows bare or dressed in light, diaphanous folds. In every detail, restraint is employed to create an elegant, yet comfortable ambience.

A balance is achieved between "authentic" country furnishings and more modern, comfortable pieces. A comfortable couch or two is usually the

OPPOSITE: Italian villas can be quite stately without undermining the charm of country living. This villa has the architectural trappings of a grand palazzo, yet the furnishings are simple and unpretentious, creating an atmosphere that is both relaxed and hospitable. Lighting plays a key role here, as thin drapes open up the space and provide panoramic views of the countryside.

BELOW: Curious antiques can be found throughout the Italian countryside. This rococo settee has a mellow, distressed finish that melds with the surroundings perfectly.

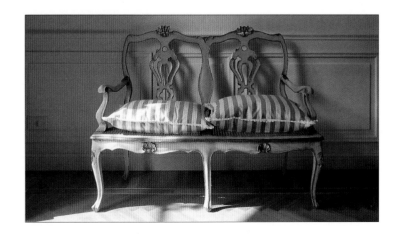

centerpiece of the room. Upholstered in sturdy fabric with soft earth tones or muted floral prints, these are arranged to create a feeling of comfort and intimacy. After all, family and friends can spend hours here chatting. Although the coffee table is a relatively modern invention, it is nevertheless found in many country retreats. A small carved *cassone*, or chest, will often do the trick, or a column pedestal or cornice can be given a glass top and used as a coffee table.

A few pieces of *mobili rustici*, or rustic furniture, go a long way toward creating a country look. Antique country furnishings were simply designed and often homemade, lending them an *arte povera* quality that has only recently become fashionable. Without much demand, the majority of country furniture has been discarded over time and is, therefore, often hard to find. For a price, of course, wonderful pieces from as early as the eighteenth century can still be bought in local shops.

The traditional Florentine table, with its ornamented hexagonal or octagonal top and carved pedestal, can be used alongside a couch or group of chairs. A *cassapanca*, which is a large chest with arms and a back, is a traditional, if not very comfortable, settee. Other Italian classics recognized more for old-world charm than comfort are folding, X-shaped Savonarola and Dante armchairs or pious *sgabello* sidechairs, all of which can be made more hospitable with a plush seat cushion.

All sense of formality is lost when the party moves outdoors. During the summer months, outdoor space is annexed as an extra room or wing of the house. No country home is complete without a portico or a pergola covered in wisteria vines leading out to the gardens. Here, the family and friends can convene in the cool shade even when the midday sun is at its peak. Often second-story bedrooms will have their own *loggie*, or covered balconies, as well.

Italian outdoor retreats meld seamlessly into nature. Stone walls reflect the mellow colors and rich texture of the surrounding landscape, as do the lichen-covered *coppi* tiles on the roof. The use of terra-cotta is nowhere more poignant than here. Patios are often lined with mossy, loosely fitted terra-cotta tiles. Terra-cotta pots and urns are everywhere, overflowing with geraniums and ivy. Stair railings

and gates are wrought iron, which weathers well, and stone balustrades are common around more stately terraces.

Dining alfresco in the countryside is any Italophile's dream come true. Many porticoes and pergolas are large enough for a long dining table, which can be anything from a simple picnic table to a more elaborate lacquered banquet. It is not uncommon for a wrought-iron table to be placed right in the garden, shaded by trees or a beautiful canvas umbrella.

ABOVE: *An open hearth provides ample heat and a lovely setting for an Alpine living room. The hooded wood mantelpiece is several centuries old. To the left of the fireplace is a lovely folk artwork painted on a wooden board. Baskets of dried flowers make attractive country decorations.*

OPPOSITE: *To insulate from both summer heat and winter cold, farmhouse walls were often made two feet (61cm) thick. Window openings were quite small and few and far between. A late Renaissance chestnut chair and desk perfectly complement this setting.*

RIGHT: *Elaborate frescoes cover the walls of many country villas outside Venice, as gifted artists could often be lured away from the city to embellish country retreats. This splendid landscape is a contemporary rendering, but certainly captures the flavor of the Renaissance. An antique birdcage adds a Victorian touch. Painted chairs hail from the eighteenth century, when Venetian artists began imitating Eastern lacquering techniques.*

ABOVE: *The symmetry of the architecture and the furnishings—not to mention the Roman bust framed against the back arch—lend this lavish portico a formal, classical air. A host of comfortable, broad-striped lounge chairs alleviates any feeling of stuffiness, and gives the space a charming appeal.*

OPPOSITE: *Authentic country antiques are hard to come by in Italy, but a few winning pieces can make a room. A chestnut trestle table is as sturdy and functional today as it was a century ago. A sgabello chair, on the other hand, is a precious find, but probably best admired from afar.*

ABOVE: *Leather-backed Dante chairs and a large antique credenza complement a carved limestone fireplace in this well-appointed living room. A collection of ancient busts and other artifacts is displayed on the mantel. In the back of the room two stone pedestals support a glass table top.*

LEFT: *Glazed terra-cotta is a centuries-old Italian tradition. Luca della Robbia glorified the art form in the fifteenth century, but by and large the practice has remained the domain of country artisans. Like all Italian folk art, glazed terra-cotta has a vast iconography and countless regional nuances. A favored medium of the* arte povera *tradition, terra-cotta crafts often have religious or allegorical themes.*

OPPOSITE: *Terra-cotta, stone, wood, and plaster are the basic ingredients of all traditional Italian homes. Country houses look and feel like fortresses because of the integrity and strength of these bulking materials, which are seldom hidden from view.* Pietra serena, *a dense, rich stone common throughout Italy, outlines the portals of this living room.*

ABOVE: *Garden furniture like this canvas reclining chair is often used indoors to create a casual look. Wooden marionettes and other folk sculptures are fun country decorations that add to the relaxed, unpretentious atmosphere. If a room is small in size, mirrors and white upholstered furnishings can be used to give the illusion of space. Trees and plants are always welcome additions to a country living room.*

LEFT: *Small living spaces rarely seem cramped in the country. Most are instead made to feel quite intimate and cozy. A few comfortable chairs and couches around the fireplace will usually suffice, as in this rustic northern living room.*

ABOVE: *A makeshift portico has a rustic quality and can be made out of just about anything. To open up the house, this portico was added by using granite pillars to hold up a simple wood canopy. Furnished with simple wrought-iron lawn furniture painted a vivid blue, the portico looks charming and—more importantly—provides a comfortable outdoor space.*

OPPOSITE: *With only a green carpet of lawn separating it from the ocean, this pergola offers cool shade and a wonderful view. The columns have been trained with flowering vines that have climbed to the canopy, which is lined with bamboo reeds. The colorful, inlaid-tile table and wicker chairs complete this summery setting.*

OPPOSITE: *Even in the mountains it gets pretty warm in the summertime, and Italians like nothing more than retreating to the pergola for lunch. Outdoor wooden furniture weathers quickly here and takes on a nice patina. Simple chairs with rush seats look charming in just about any country setting, indoors or out.*

RIGHT: *A terrace garden is the perfect place to set even the most formal table. A little shade is nice, of course, so pick a spot at least partially covered by a tree.*

ABOVE: *The portico of this renovated farmhouse is remarkable for its muscular archi-tecture. The integrity of the construction—the fine masonry and brickwork—imbues the space with a stalwart character. The simple architecture can afford tasteful, modern lighting fixtures. Terra-cotta planters accent the building's earth tones.*

ABOVE: *Lichen-covered stone walls have a special poignancy in the Italian countryside. They often seem to be as timeless and stoic as the land itself. This wall fronts a stately Tuscan villa.*

LEFT: *Ivy trims the entire length of this Alpine house and gives this portico a rustic countenance. White-washed walls and green shutters complement these ivy "whiskers" nicely, while red plaid curtains in the kitchen look picture-perfect next to bunches of impatiens.*

LEFT: *Artfully stenciled walls give this spectacular view a run for its money. Subtle pastels give the interior a warm glow, while large windows usher in the countryside's natural beauty. With views like these, a room needs little else to be fully furnished.*

BELOW: *A brace of delicate French doors opens off this grand rotunda, bringing the countryside right into the living room. The inlaid floor and classical wall moldings complement both the shape and proportions of the room. Plump couches make this formal setting quite comfortable and welcoming.*

RIGHT: *Capri's sprawling downtown makes an interesting mosaic from a neighboring hillside pergola. The dappled shade of the vine-covered trellis is a nice place to take in the view and enjoy dining alfresco. Fanciful wrought-iron chairs seem to imitate the tendrils creeping along the pergola.*

BELOW: *Color is an important element in outdoor table setting. The colors of the natural landscape seem to have an especially buoyant effect on the Italian table. Here, navy-rimmed china and a sky blue tablecloth are accented by yellow-cushioned chairs and red flowers placed at each setting.*

ABOVE: *Large, glassed-in archways make this living room a country paradise. Indeed, when sitting on one of the plush couches, one has the feeling of being outdoors. With ivy trained along the arches inside, the window panes do not seem to stem the encroaching wilderness. The room's subtle white and cream palette is cool and serene.*

ABOVE: *The quality of light at dusk can be quite evocative throughout the Italian countryside. This partially covered loggia offers a great view of an especially surreal twilight. The architecture is simple and seems to acquiesce to the profound beauty of the landscape. The massive walls emphasize the lyric quality of the slender wrought-iron chairs.*

OPPOSITE: *The Italian coastline offers many spectacular vistas, but none more stunning than the one from this cliff-top portico. The structure provides shelter from the sun without taking away from the view. The horizontal, clean lines of the architecture are mirrored by those of the furniture, which is simple and solidly built.*

BED AND BATH

Life in the Italian countryside is all about enjoying time spent with family and friends. The intimacies of the kitchen and living rooms and the beautiful vastness of the outdoors set the stage for relaxed, lazy days and nights passed eating and drinking, talking and socializing. Life is very much removed from the pressures of the modern world, and country dwellers appreciate the chance to visit and be together.

The bedroom, therefore, is not the prime focus of the country retreat, as the sparseness of the decor may suggest. In the Italian countryside, the bedroom is basically just that—a room with a bed—and it is used primarily for sleeping. Here, especially, a few finely made pieces of furniture suffice. The bedroom is generally not a nest feathered for private escape, for the attraction of the country home lies elsewhere.

Which is not to say the bedroom isn't quaint and comfortable—it is both. The sense of uncluttered space is a luxury in itself. The openness allows the architecture of the room to feature prominently. Often the roofline and exposed rafters create an unusual canopy. The ceiling and beams are traditionally whitewashed with lime. Walls are painted off-white or another warm, muted color. The floors are dark stained wood or worn stone and are rarely carpeted. A few throw rugs can soften the effect of the bare floors without taking away from the clean lines of the space.

The single most prominent piece of furniture is, of course, the bed. In the master bedroom, the *letto matrimoniale*, or matrimonial bed, has an elaborate headbord usually made of carved wood or sculpted iron. In stately country villas, these are often quite fancy displays of craftsmanship, the wood carved and gilded in magnificent relief.

The *baldacchino*, or canopy bed, is still popular in rural settings, if for no other reason than to protect the sleeper from flaking whitewash. But they are beautiful too. The Tyrolean bed, with its heavy, carved, painted wooden canopy, is a magnificent find in many villas in the northern Alps. These enormous beds can afford rich velvet or brocaded drapes—the better for keeping warm in the winter months. In Tuscany and Umbria, baldachins are usually cast in slender wrought iron, which can be lyrically embellished but which is more often crafted in sleek rectilinear forms. These canopies are left bare or are draped in lightweight linens with a soft, neutral color. Either way, the clean lines of the bed are

OPPOSITE: *Although the process of stenciling the plaster walls of this bedroom was complex and labor-intensive, the finished effect is astonishing. Furnishings are few, enhancing the setting by not taking away from the ornate wall design.*

preserved. Further south, Spanish influence is evident in the ornately carved and turned four-poster beds, which are distinguished by their spiraling balustrades. According to Italian tradition, a religious painting or symbol crowned with a small olive branch hangs over most beds to protect the sleeper.

Bed linens, like table linens, are possessions worthy of investment. Italy is home to some of the world's most famous linen manufacturers, and quality bedding is a mark of distinction. In the country, bed linens are notable not only for their exceptional quality, but also for their simple design and subtle texture. Dust ruffles and frilly shams and bedcovers do not appeal to the Italian sense of line and space.

Other bedroom furnishings are few. Massive wood *armadi*, or wardrobes, are great for storing clothes. They are plainly carved and often decorated with nail studs or other simple hardware. In the northern regions, commodes and wardrobes are often lacquered and painted in floral or narrative motifs of the *arte povera* tradition. Italians are famous for the organization of their closet space, so what can't be stored in the *armadio* will most likely be secreted away behind closed doors. A *cassone*, or large chest, can be found in just about any room in an Italian farmhouse, but it is especially useful in the bedroom for storing bed linens or blankets.

Italian country villas and farmhouses are not famous for their plumbing. Until recently, it was not unusual to find *case coloniche* without running water, and what we consider standard bathroom fixtures today were not so standard in the Italian countryside a short time ago. Not surprisingly, therefore, bathrooms in converted farmhouses and restored villas are usually rather modern.

The best way to maintain traditional country decor in the bathroom is by using traditional country materials. As in every other room of the house, terra-cotta tiles or hardwood can be used with great effect on bathroom floors and walls. Locally crafted ceramic tiles bring regional flavor—as well as color—to shower and washbasin areas. Details such as a hand-forged iron towel bar or an original stone or marble sink can make all the difference.

ABOVE: *Many Alpine bedrooms are endowed with enormous hooded hearths. Graced with such a prominent architectural element, the bedroom does not require much decoration. Bare plaster walls impart a great sense of texture, and a few Persian rugs can soften the effect of hardwood floors. Shutters inside and out preclude the need for curtains.*

LEFT: *A room with a view is a rare luxury, yet this room has a superb vista. The loggia of the upstairs bedroom is covered with a bamboo lattice. Downstairs, sliding shutter doors open onto a tiled terrace garden. With such inspiring views, the bedroom decor can well afford simplicity. A sumptuous settee completes the setting.*

ABOVE: *Hanging on an Alpine bedroom wall, tyke-size ski poles and skis make a quaint allusion to halcyon days of youth. A few well-chosen furnishings coordinating with the dark exposed wood ceiling beams give a rustic touch to the spare decor.*

ABOVE: *A massive, ornately carved antique crib is the centerpiece of this nursery. With such a singular furnishing, all that's needed to complete the room are a few finely crafted wood toys. The design is spare and sophisticated, but it is also imbued with enough fantasy to inspire any child's imagination.*

OPPOSITE: *High-pitched roofs often make for interesting interior spaces. Ceiling beams jut into this bedroom at wild angles, creating dramatic volumes. These sloped wood ceilings are beautiful not only for their rich, grainy texture, but also for their simple, purposeful construction.*

RIGHT: *If all bedrooms opened onto balconies overlooking the Italian countryside, decorating would be easy. Floral-print curtains and delicate French doors frame this room's lush vista. The walls and bedcovers are finely textured but plainly decorated, designed not to detract from the room's natural beauty.*

LEFT: *From botanical prints on the walls to floral-patterned bedcovers and drapes, a country bedroom looks perfectly quaint outfitted in bright colorful flowers. Coordinating these colors— from lamp shades to ceiling beams— gives the room a finished look. Lyrically embellished wrought-iron beds have an organic quality that follows the theme.*

OPPOSITE: *Country artisans are well trained in the art of trompe l'oeil embellishment. Hanging flower garlands and sprightly vines are painted on the walls and ceiling of this bedroom in Tuscany. The brass beds accent the gold tassels painted on the walls. Although the window is small and narrow, the long, broad curtains make it seem larger.*

ABOVE: *Nothing imparts rustic charm to a bedroom like a hand-patched quilt. Throw one on a bed and the room is immediately transformed. This bedroom happens to be well rusticated already, outfitted as it is with red gingham-covered footstools and side tables. Short candlestick lamps bring diminutive cuteness to the setting, as do miniature botanical prints. The eighteenth-century bed is opulently carved, the headboard inlaid with a glazed ceramic portrait of the Virgin Mary.*

OPPOSITE: *In the country bathroom, a single antique can make the entire room wash. This combination mirror and toiletry drawer is just such a piece. Functional and attractive, its scalloped edges and decorative palings and finials bring a new dimension to the room's straight lines and flat surfaces.*

LEFT, TOP: *Straight lines and smooth surfaces are the cornerstones of Italian design, and the bathroom is where these attributes are most apparent. Strong lighting is essential, and quality fixtures—chrome faucets, for example—can greatly enhance the bathroom decor. Lyric embellishments like a wrought-iron hat rack and a carved wooden screen complement the rigid linearity of the bathroom.*

LEFT, BOTTOM: *In the Italian Alps, diamond-shaped window mullions are commonly used and suggest an Austrian influence. As elsewhere throughout the Italian countryside, the palette here is subdued and earthy. Woodwork is generally dark, and terra-cotta floors and plaster walls are favored. A white-on-white embroidered bedspread and cream-colored canopy and curtains highlight the texture of the architectural elements.*

OPPOSITE: *Thatch roofs are uncommon in Italy, but this renovated farmhouse is none the worse for wear. Wrought-iron beds are a staple throughout the central region, and many antiques are fancifully embellished. Italian appreciation for clean lines and uncluttered space prompts bedcovers to be neatly tucked under the mattress.*

LEFT: *Bedroom furnishings are often the most rustic of all household belongings. Ponderous, knotted-wood beds and a peg-leg stool are classic country fare. They seem wellsuited to a room with split and splintered roof beams. A vase of fresh cut flowers makes a weekend sojourn in the country special.*

OPPOSITE: *With a terrace garden and lofty courtyard view, this villa bedroom is splendidly decadent. Hand-painted French doors lead to a balcony with Gothic carved-stone balustrades. One can almost feel the gentle breeze wafting the smell of gardenias through lustrous folds of damask.*

RIGHT: *Italians are renowned for systematic, orderly interiors, and the bathroom is no exception. The Italian bathroom, in fact, sets the standard for spatial economy. The well-appointed washroom has myriad shelves, drawers, and cabinets. Rustic charm, however, is not lost in the woodwork.*

Part Three

ENGLISH COUNTRY

INTRODUCTION

Of all the great things that the English have invented and made part of the credit of the national character, the most perfect, the most characteristic, the only one they have mastered completely in all its details so that it becomes a compendious illustration of their social genius and their manners, is the well appointed, well administered, well filled country house.

—Henry James

If you are like me, Beatrix Potter's tales of Peter Rabbit or Frances Hodgson Burnett's *The Secret Garden* gave you your first impression of an English country house. Illustrations of both Mr. McGregor's humble farmhouse and vegetable garden, and Mary and Colin's Misselthwaite Manor with butlers, nannies, and a mysterious walled-in garden gave me an early feeling for the relationship between an English country house and its surroundings. Whether great in size and provenance, with an exquisitely designed garden of climbing roses and clipped boxwoods, or simple in stature and plainly picturesque, the relationship between the English country house and garden represents an essential aspect of English country life.

While the English country house and garden are the center of English country life, the family is the true heart of English country style. In the film adaptation of Jane Austen's *Sense and Sensibility*, the luxurious atmosphere of the Dashwoods' mansion evokes the idea of family because the rooms were created by the family's ancestral heritage. Generations of the privileged Dashwood family lived in the same house, creating layer upon layer of years of collections. A combination of architectural styles, decorating styles, furniture, and objects filled the rooms and gave the family a connection to their heritage. When Mrs. Dashwood and her daughters had to leave their estate and move into a smaller home, they were leaving more than just their house. By moving they were actually leaving a part of their family behind.

English country houses usually reveal their great age and have less than perfect interiors. Even in the wealthiest household, upholstery might be faded, painted surfaces dulled by the patina of age, and spaces crammed with old furniture and objects. There is a casual commingling of periods, styles, patterns, and colors. Well-chosen furniture, fabrics, and accessories show an appreciation for the antique. A

OPPOSITE: *A thatched-roof cottage in the Cotswolds defines the English ideal of a country retreat because of the way it is integrated into its rural surroundings. Climbing ivy adds to the overall effect.*

combination of shabbiness and luxury is the true nature of English country style decorating.

Masculine-looking book-lined walls make up libraries, and drawing rooms with a feminine feel are arranged with fine period furniture and decorated with gold-framed oil portrait paintings and yards of chintz fabrics. Ornamented fireplace mantels are presided over by classical busts and Chinese porcelains, and windows give views onto improbably vast and luxurious expanses of green lawns—all ideals of English country style.

TO THE MANOR BORN:
THE HISTORY OF THE ENGLISH COUNTRY HOUSE

In the Middle Ages, the English country house was built as a testament to a family's power and prestige. Passed down through the first-born male line, the country house symbolized the continuity of established families who resided in the same house for generations. It was typically filled with portraits of family, powerful friends, monarchs, and classical heroes.

In the centuries following the Renaissance, an essential part of a young gentleman's education was to take an extensive sight-seeing European Grand Tour, during which he would collect large amounts of objects and furniture. These would serve as reminders of his trip when he returned to England. Classical busts, oil paintings of great classical scenes, marble inlay tables, tapestries, carpets, furniture, blue and

R I G H T : *An English country living room is both elegant and cozy, stylized and eclectic. Turquoise-colored walls enliven the room's somber beige patterned upholstery and carpeting. An identical pair of sofas strewn with throw pillows sits fireside. A built-in book shelf has an unusual Art Deco–style pediment and enshrines groupings of china plates, vases, bowls, and figurines. Framed pictures defy the laws of gravity, hanging flat against the slanted wall.*

white porcelains, and even architectural drawings to use to create his country manor were the souvenirs of his jaunts. In combination with new, well-chosen pieces of quality and style, these souvenirs comprise the collections found in great English country houses today.

The vast economic and social changes wrought by the Industrial Revolution led to urbanization and the growth of a prosperous middle class. By the mid-nineteenth century, the country house was a refuge from fast-paced London life. The country house offered an escape from the city and an opportunity to cultivate leisure time. Hunting and fishing, drawing and painting, and musical pursuits, literature, games, and eating, as well as afternoon tea with biscuits and jam, fox hunts, and polo matches typify the activities enjoyed at the country house.

The grand style of the wealthiest English country households was determined by the current fashion of the period. The latest architectural developments, imported fabrics, and furniture were sought with a fervor. The lifestyles of the wealthiest were eagerly adopted by the merely affluent, and it is these humbler versions of the grand country manors that truly reflect the grace and charm that is the hallmark of the great English country house.

Today, the National Trust owns and preserves many of England's oldest, most impressive country houses. Often these properties are museumlike—completely preserved encapsulations of the era of manservants, housemaids, and footmen. Their legacy, however, the time-honored style known as "English Country"—is much more liveable. In the pages that follow, you will find numerous examples of this comfortable, eclectic, lived-in style that so perfectly combines past and present—and may inspire you to create your own version of English Country.

A B O V E : *A functional stainless steel sink sits atop recycled barn siding for a true farmhouse effect. The chipped paint and crumble-down look is enhanced by fresh-cut wildflowers in an old clay pitcher. Potted geraniums catch sunlight from a window with a garden view that brightens the task of dishwashing.*

ABOVE: *A vaulted glass ceiling provides a generous amount of sunlight for the healthy growth of flowering vines. The bright, patterned fabric on a round central table and easy chairs echoes the floral theme of the room and adds a splash of color. Extra seating is provided in the form of mismatched wooden chairs casually placed around the table.*

HOUSE AND GARDEN

The English country house comes in many variations of style and size. Regal greystone manors sit majestically atop green meadows. Large classical structures with a regular pattern of windows and a large portico reflect Italian palazzos, while towering masses of half-timbered walls, thatched roofs, and diamond-mullioned windows are indicative of classic cottage style. Organic building materials such as brick, stone, stucco, and wood together with thatched roofs and decorative wisps of climbing ivy combine to make these houses look as if they were carved out of the lush English countryside.

England's verdant countryside has spawned generations of passionate gardeners, and cultivation of the exteriors of country houses has become an art form. Embellishments of climbing vines and flowers further integrate country houses into the landscape. The classic image of a country cottage with roses adorning the front door can be found on both the grandest manor house and the humblest thatched cottage. This combination of natural building materials and natural adornments establishes for the architecture a feeling of oneness with nature.

Avid travelers, the English have brought home many great ideas from other cultures and adapted them to their own. Inspirations from France and Italy led to England's grand-style symmetrical gardens. Grottos, picturesque vistas, fake ruins, pergolas, and manmade ponds set around circuitous paths set the standard for English garden design. Ideas were also imported to the country from the city and further adapted to fit the lifestyle of the country—the idea of melding architecture and nature together started not in the country but in London.

Indoor/outdoor spaces such as patios and porches are essential to English country living as they provide the opportunity to enjoy gardens and the countryside within a semi-enclosed, private space. Lounging the afternoon away on a wisteria-covered patio on a lazy summer day, or dining in a glass conservatory that stretches out into magnificent gardens are just a couple of the many true pleasures of English country living.

OPPOSITE: *A Georgian-style brick manor house majestically presides over idyllic estate grounds. The house's reflection on the water complements both architecture and nature.*

RIGHT: *An inviting two-story classic cottage has a thatched roof with opposing chimneys whose fireplaces are used to warm both sides of the cozy house. A central front door is embellished with an arched trellis that helps support the generous climbing vines that decorate the façade.*

ABOVE: *The front of a country house of classic Palladian proportions is completely covered with creeping vines. The freshly painted white windows and front door show that the vines are the deliberately unclipped embellishments of an otherwise well-maintained manor.*

ABOVE: *An English garden bursts with a complementary mix of flora in bright colors. Backed by a privet hedge, the combination of pink, raspberry, violet, yellow, and orange blossoms creates a joyful display.*

RIGHT: *A privet hedge is pierced by a picket gate and an arched trellis with red climbing roses. The low-hung gate allows a view into the enclosed, enchanting garden.*

BELOW: The hard edges of a tall, mullioned window are softened by outlines of English wisteria. A family's heraldry appears in the geometric design of the windowpanes to identify the houses's original residents.

ABOVE: *The owner's green thumb has made a simple stone cottage romantic and inviting. A lush front border garden is presided over by the bright red flowers of climbing vines and hanging container plants. The cottage's many windows give its inhabitants a connection to the outside.*

ABOVE: *A teak bench with a curvilinear design is situated for its unobstructed view of a terraced backyard. A wicker basket used to carry the accoutrements of a busy gardener is filled with fresh-cut flowers and a wide-brimmed hat.*

LEFT: *A hexagonal brick folly was originally built as a hunting lodge or getaway cottage on the grounds of a large manor. Hipped-roof projections add space to the interior. Blue-painted windows and door add visual interest and create a contrast between the red bricks and green grass.*

RIGHT: *Matisse painted trees like these, their slender beauty providing a supremely elegant backdrop for a simple arrangement of French iron garden chairs around a square outdoor table. The harmony between the brick terraces and manicured hedges can be appreciated from the garden furnishings used as a stop-off during strolling or working in this pastoral setting.*

RIGHT: *A charming pavilion, newly erected for secluded outdoor entertaining, provides visitors with a covered venue for contemplation of a manicured backyard. A terrace is created by a sloping stone wall behind a low-growing bed of foliage. New trees were planted for future generations to enjoy.*

ABOVE: *A manor house's façade was designed with a balanced arrangement of windows set neatly within unembellished stone walls. Informal-style landscaping surrounds the house and connects it to the surrounding countryside.*

ABOVE: *A conservatory pulsating with life is filled with plants, flowers, and Victorian-style wicker and iron furniture. Natural woven shades block the strong sun of high noon and can be rolled up as the day goes on. A terra-cotta floor allows for easy cleanup of water spills and of the grass and dirt that are inevitably dragged in from the outside.*

ABOVE: *A simple stone cottage has an interesting Moorish-style pediment on stylized columns. The plain landscaping and the pureness of the façade have the appeal of modern-day minimalism.*

RIGHT: *A typical English country cottage, the strongly graphic feel of this house and outbuilding contrasts with its informally landscaped setting. A front yard moat is crossed by a covered bridge with a second story to match the height of the main house.*

ROOMS FOR COMFORTABLE LIVING

English country style interiors may not always appear to be organized, but underlying the seemingly undisciplined mix of periods, patterns, and colors are principles of balance and harmony. The result is an overall attractive and comfortable impression. You may find such natural elements as flagstone floors; woven natural floor matting; half-timbered and brick walls; and fabrics of cotton, wool and silk. Colors of the earth, from russet reds to deep leafy greens, the pale yellows of flowers, and light sky blues brighten English country style rooms. Patterns inspired by nature show up on fabric, porcelain, carpets, and wall stencils, bringing the garden indoors. Walls may feature hunting prints, landscape paintings, or Victorian etchings, all layered atop a floral wallpaper.

The charm and timelessness of English country style endure because the best rooms of this style all pay great attention to detail. From the tiniest tassel to the plumpest sofa, from fresh-cut flowers to a fruit still-life in a blue and white porcelain bowl, the details of English country style are paramount. John Fowler of Colefax & Fowler, the most influential decorator of the English country house look, was known for his unmatched attention to decorative and architectural detail. He developed an exquisite balance of color, pattern, and fantasy in his English country style rooms, which is probably why these rooms are as celebrated today as when they were first created.

The attention to detail begins in the front hall, the introduction to a house. Its importance dates from the Middle Ages when it served wealthy families as reception room, living room, and dining hall. A family's heraldry and armor were displayed as embellishment and as an announcement of identity. Tapestries were hung to display wealth and to insulate the hall from drafts. Later, the development of wooden wainscoting for insulation provided a backdrop for the minimal furnishings of boards on trestles and benches, which were used for easy setup and removal from the multifunctional space.

In later years, the great hall remained the center of the English country house, but the need for privacy led to the addition of private second-floor quarters with drawing rooms for intimate meetings. Over centuries, the layout of the house changed from a large central hall into a collection of rooms on separate floors. From this arrangement developed the classic country house layout of a living room and dining

OPPOSITE: *A multilayered decorating scheme reflects additions made over time in this living room. A mixing of unrelated patterns and styles and a jumble of various accessories throughout defines this room's eclectic style. Draped plaid fabric over the table top and sofa has a homespun appeal.*

room flanking a central hall with bedrooms and bathrooms upstairs. Over time, separate hallways, libraries, galleries, and drawing rooms were added for the comfort of country house inhabitants.

In today's country house, the front hallway retains its importance for setting a welcoming tone for guests. It is usually furnished with restraint and a sense of formality, with attention to its practical function. The English weather is tracked in through both front and back doors, and a place to sit and remove boots, a stand in which to stow umbrellas, and a rack on which to hang coats are important features. Hardwood, flagstone, brick, tiled, or slate floors are common. Walls may be white or painted plaster, half-paneled, wallpapered, and hung with pictures. Furniture is usually kept to a minimum. A console table with matching chairs may be surmounted by a large mirror, and provides a good surface on which to toss mail and keys.

The English country living room provides a refuge for leisurely pursuits and common functions of the house. In smaller houses, the living room may also include a small dining area, and be lined with bookshelves if a separate library does not exist. An overall timeless feeling of comfort and relaxation is created by a casual mixing of complementary fabric patterns and colors, set within the unifying influence of a harmonious color scheme. Old furniture predominates and mixes with well-chosen new pieces. Sun-faded window treatments and tattered upholstery add lived-in charm. The focus of the living room is often the central fireplace. Furniture and objects balanced around the fireplace add grace and harmonize disparate pieces into the scheme.

The final design touch in the English country room is often a collection of cherished objects. Continually added-to collections and objects with meaning, inherited or newly acquired, create tabletop displays, make a statement about an owner's style, and will probably become treasured heirlooms.

ABOVE: *A neatly furnished hallway leads outdoors to a flagstone terrace and the garden beyond. Walking sticks fill an umbrella stand next to a unique wooden side chair. A classic English equestrian oil painting hangs above the wainscoting on available wall space. An heirloom grandfather clock's case reveals the fine grain of its highly polished veneer.*

ABOVE: *An exposed beam ceiling with whitewashed walls pierced by diamond-mullioned leaded windows makes a quaint backdrop for an informal living room. The antique style of the new sofa is lent authenticity by time-worn and faded upholstery. Muted color, decorative fringe, and cording enrich the comfortable furnishings.*

ABOVE: *A quietly elegant entryway is tastefully decorated with a neat display of stylish brimmed hats and an arrangement of walking sticks and umbrellas in an oversized urn. Hanging binoculars anticipate the next birdwatching trip. Coats and boots are kept behind a closet door fitted with medieval-style hardware.*

BELOW: *A Gothic castle becomes a work of art in itself when framed by this deep-set, arched doorway in this English country home. An antique birdcage is a delicate touch.*

ABOVE: *An absence of strong patterns or colors in this room emphasizes objects and furnishings and helps to create a fresh living environment. In the spirit of English country decorating, three blue-and-white platters draw attention to the room's high ceiling. Other collected pieces decorate a table on which keys and mail may be tossed.*

ABOVE: *A painted cabinet houses a country collection of table linens and is conveniently positioned for outdoor dining and picnic use. The color of the cabinet is echoed by a harmony of complementary objects and artwork hung on the white plaster and exposed stone wall.*

LEFT: *The purposefully casual arrangement of slipcovered furniture creates an undecorated feeling for comfort in this spacious living room. Peripheral areas are filled with bookshelves, tables, and writing desks which show the many functions of the accommodating space. An ancestral portrait presides majestically over the fireplace.*

OPPOSITE: *Natural woven seagrass matting, celadon wainscoting, and built-ins create a fresh looking library. A large slipcovered ottoman in beige and cream is used as a coffee table and for storage of more reading material. The "less is more" decorating approach brings a relaxed airiness to the well-filled space, and keeps the books the focus of the room.*

TOP, RIGHT: *Sometimes an English country house is not large enough to accommodate a separate library. Here, a makeshift library was created in a small outbuilding when a leather bookshelf border was nailed on the edge of a farmhouse table and shelves overstuffed with books were added.*

BOTTOM, RIGHT: *Virtually all available space is filled in this combination hallway and library. A sofa crosses the doorway, thus connecting two rooms and making them one. Spillover shelves store a vast collection of books.*

LEFT: *The real accoutrements of an active English country life inhabit the back entrance area of this home. An ever-evolving utilitarian space hosts rubber wellies, firewood, garden clippers, and a hand-basket for weekend chores, along with the large house's impressive set of keys.*

OPPOSITE: *Garden style gives an entryway its decorating theme. Framed botanical prints and terra-cotta pots filled with flowers and topiaries grace the space. A vine border, floral-patterned curtain treatment, and woven seagrass floor matting complete the verdant motif.*

OPPOSITE: *A balanced display of skirted tables with matching accessories and hanging pictures flanks a Tudor-style fireplace with a carved overhead decoration that organizes the great room. An oversized ottoman upholstered in tapestry and a sofa with a matching pair of throw pillows sit on an Aubusson carpet that enriches the space with its coloration and formidable size.*

TOP, RIGHT: *Furniture and personal objects, including a rolltop desk, dried flowers, and antique prints, enrich this space. A plain beige wall-to-wall carpet is enhanced by a worn needlepoint rug of great character and charm.*

BOTTOM, RIGHT: *Outfitted for the realistic features of English country life, the flagstone floor of an entryway hall provides for the trudging in of rain- or mud-soaked boots. Umbrellas are conveniently stowed doorside. Candle lanterns provide illumination when the door is closed and at night, as well as antique charm.*

RIGHT: *A cool white living room is decked out in a blue and white color scheme. A shabby-chic sofa is covered with a faded checkerboard quilt and strewn with square throw pillows of coordinating patterns. Gold accents warm the room and imbue it with a sense of glamour. It is this combination of comfort and elegance that defines the English country ideal.*

BELOW: *In this cozy living room, well-coordinated mismatched fabrics cover worn-out furnishings and flea market finds serve to imbue the decor with charm.*

OPPOSITE: *A plush Chesterfield creates an inviting backdrop for three neatly placed throw pillows of uniform size. The high windowsill is a good stage for a balanced display of heirloom statuettes. A single vase of fresh flowers echoes the porcelain flower arrangement under a glass dome and breathes life into the decor.*

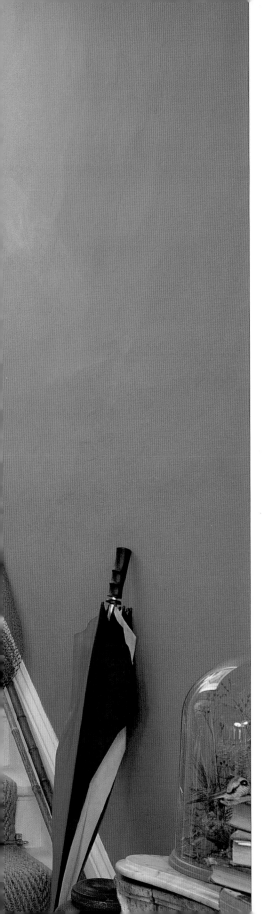

The paraphernalia of sport and daily life inhabit this warmly colored hallway. A passion for birds and butterflies is evident from the objects preserved under glass.

ABOVE: *A larger sized country house still has housebells, once used to summon servants, left over from its grand past. To avoid confusion and ensure prompt attention, each room had its own bell.*

LEFT: *The walls of this staircase are papered in a two-tone beige-striped pattern and hung with a large series of simply framed bird prints that invoke a country feel. The wide-stripe pattern reinforces the verticality of the walls and double height of the ceiling.*

LEFT: *A balustraded stairway landing is a large enough space in which to position an antique carved table. In addition to its ornamental purpose, the table is a wonderful surface to display a flower arrangement held in a classic Arts and Crafts ceramic vase.*

A B O V E : *The center of an informal living room plays host to an oversized tufted settee with a rolled back. Upholstered in pale floral cotton chintz with a twisted silk cord, the settee adds romantic quirkiness to the rural interior.*

237

ABOVE: *A matching pair of table lamps and paintings on both sides of a window help to structure a large home office and sitting room, but the seemingly unorganized mix of furniture gives the feeling that the space is filled with the leftovers of a very large household.*

ABOVE: *A floor-to-ceiling window presides over a subtly dramatic room built to look like an old manor house. Exposed beams and stone pierce the plaster walls, creating a rustic ambience. Simple furnishings and accessories accent the "lodge" feel of the space.*

LEFT: *An invitingly comfortable living room is traditionally appointed with upholstered furniture in coordinating patterns and colors. Various floral patterns on the throw pillows and window treatments, and on the ottoman that serves as a coffee table, connect with each other to unify the room. The blue easy chair is a cool contrast to the warm-hued upholstery set against enveloping yellow walls.*

RIGHT: *A montage of black-and-white engravings and small oil paintings creates a focal point on a sunflower yellow sitting room wall. A mix of textile patterns having a predominantly red color scheme enriches the dark grain of the wood furniture and handsome desk clock.*

ABOVE: *An enormous second-story window reveals an estate's well-manicured grounds and the breathtaking mountainous coastline. The window itself is a work of art—no curtains or other embellisments are needed to enhance its beauty.*

KITCHENS AND DINING ROOMS

In the earliest English country houses, meals were ceremoniously presented to the family in the great hall, which also functioned as the dining room. Formal presentation rituals are still performed today, and the idea of ceremony still exists, even in middle class country houses: dinner guests and family members are expected to dress when dinner is served in the main dining room.

As times changed, dining in smaller parties became more desirable, as it was an honor to be selected to share a meal with a small party. Instead of dining in the great hall, the meal was served at a small gateleg table in a corner of the living room. Today's smaller country houses may not always have the luxury of a separate dining room. In modest houses, a scrubbed pine table in a corner of the kitchen will be used instead. In slightly larger houses, dining rooms adjacent to the kitchen that were built originally for servants are used. They may be furnished with ordinary pieces arranged in a practical, rather than fancy, manner.

Formal dining rooms used mostly for entertaining retain a place of importance in the house. A large oak table surrounded by a matching suite of chairs is the focal point of the room. A sideboard is used as a buffet surface, and a tall breakfront houses the family's china and table linens. A silver tea set and candlesticks decorate tabletops and add a touch of glamour to the room. Paintings, mirrors, matching pairs of wall sconces, and plates adorn walls. Often a beautiful crystal chandelier hangs over the table. An oriental rug, patterned carpet, or natural woven matting is an appropriate covering for a hardwood floor, while damask draperies may serve to accent windows.

In medieval country houses, kitchens were mostly separate from the formal dining area. Meals were cooked over open fires and the kitchen would often become too sooty and greasy in which to dine comfortably. To help ventilation, these rooms were built with high ceilings.

Today, the kitchen is the hub of the English country house. Besides being the place where a family's food is prepared, family and friends often relax here to share meals and sip tea. Regardless of size, English country kitchens always display a well-organized use of space often including natural pine or painted wood fitted cabinets for maximum storage. If more room is needed, there will often be a separate

OPPOSITE: *Trompe l'oeil sheaves of wheat painted around the mantel create a focal point in this dining room. The pale blue mantelpiece complements the color of checked cushions that soften the hardness of wooden chairs. Blue and white china set out for serving matches a small collection on a round side table.*

pantry or scullery to house washers and dryers, a freezer, and more shelving for storing food and tools. A scrubbed pine table is the focal point of many country kitchens and windows are usually hung with gingham or other homespun fabric curtains.

Built-in open shelving and plate racks display large collections of hanging cups, pitchers, plates, and platters. Baskets hanging from the ceiling next to dried herbs, a rectangular pine table with a bouquet of fresh-cut wildflowers, and a suite of painted wooden chairs with rush seats are classic embellishments. Matching window treatments and seat cushions help tie a kitchen's decorative scheme together and unify the environment of disparate tools and objects.

The Aga cooker is often the heart of the English country kitchen and is visually appropriate where modern appliances like refrigerators and dishwashers are best hidden behind cabinet doors. The Aga provides a variety of cooking facilities, as well as a place for drying wet laundry, and possibly heating most of the house's radiators. The Aga may be powered by gas, oil, or electricity, and comes in many different sizes and a broad range of bright enameled colors to coordinate with any scheme.

ABOVE: *The diamond pattern of exterior leaded windows as seen through more contemporary window panes creates a feeling of the past mixing with the present—typical of English country style. Scrubbed wood countertops coordinate with the interior window set in a pure white plaster wall. Only unfinished wood and natural-toned objects exist within the picturesque kitchen.*

OPPOSITE: *Butcher-block countertops are conveniently situated beneath a window providing a brightly lit workspace. A hint of a rectangular washbasin is seen opposite an Aga that matches the creamy color of the walls. Green tiles, a traditional surface material, cover the lower portion of the wall and introduce color to the room. Colorful pots are displayed as decorative elements as well as for practical accessibility.*

LEFT: *Eighteenth-century mahogany chairs, a dining table for eight, gold-framed oil portraits, and well-chosen decorative accessories comprise this dining room painted an unusual shade of deep teal. A red velvet upholstered easy chair with a standing floor lamp coordinates with the warm color of the curtains, but is a curious addition to an otherwise traditionally furnished room.*

ABOVE: *Ice blue combines with natural tones to create an eclectic, yet harmonious feel in this country kitchen.*

ABOVE: *A whimsical procession of mounted horses and hunting dogs parades above the architrave in a double-height dining room flooded with natural sunlight. Sky-blue walls echo the clear sky above. The red tablecloth provides a warm contrast to the coolness of the cobalt blue chairs and coordinates with the adjacent sun-bathed living room.*

ABOVE: *A neo-Gothic style conservatory makes a dramatic setting for a warm-weather dining room. Two sets of double doors lead outside to a private terrace surrounded by thick foliage where the fresh flowers that embellish the table were cut. The green and white plaid seat cushions on iron dining chairs and matching tablecloth echo the color scheme of the outdoors.*

OPPOSITE: *A display of mostly white objects in a well-designed, all-cream compact kitchen is strategic for maximizing the sense of space. Glass canisters neatly display flour, sugar, and other foodstuffs on organized shelves. A pristine white tea service is set up for the traditional English afternoon ritual.*

RIGHT: *In the corner of a rustic alley kitchen, shelves display utilitarian equipment and food. Airtight containers and apothecary jars provide see-through storage of food staples. Cutting boards, pots, pans, and rolling pins are set underneath the wood countertop for easy access.*

ABOVE: *A pristine country kitchen's creamy yellow cupboards and door create the backdrop for a sturdy table and antique wood chairs. A restrained use of accessories evokes a lived-in quality without seeming cluttered. Cookbooks, potted plants, and glasses are openly displayed, breaking up the regularity and modern look of wood-fronted cabinets.*

ABOVE: *An informal country kitchen is embellished with collections of the practical objects used there. A hanging display of linens, platters, and plates and a suite of covered pots coordinate with a prevailing blue-and-white color scheme. The table is spread with a white linen tablecloth and the chairs are relaxed with soft blue-and-white-check seat cushions. An old hearth is a nook for a glass-fronted storage cabinet that holds cookbooks and the family's china.*

ABOVE: *Balloon-back dining chairs, heirloom-style table linens, and antique furniture set within the muted colors of an adjoining living room and dining room create an old-world atmosphere. A traditionally set dining table befits the graceful interior.*

OPPOSITE: *The great age of this country house reveals the progressive use of a hallway over time. Designed and decorated as a formal passageway, this hall has a Palladian window and arched pediment. Gold-framed portraits hung gallery-style on paneled walls make for an impressive entrance to the dining room. Both the masonry floor in slight disrepair and the faded upholstery of the chairs express a casual attitude. Everyday objects adorning a small table further evidence that the hall is no longer exclusively used as walk-through space.*

ABOVE

a match

plaster b

and cer

E

h

r

o

t

c

e

a

BELOW: *The close proximity of a dining area to the adjacent kitchen suggests that it is privately used by the homeowners rather than reserved for formal entertaining. A casual mixing of greens on the walls, moldings, chairs, and tablecloth unifies the room in a relaxed style. An eclectic mix of objects—terra-cotta pots, candlesticks and a teapot on the mantel, a hanging empty birdcage, and paintings resting on the molding—shows a casual country decorating approach.*

ABOVE: *Creative use of available space sets this four-oven Aga neatly under the rounded Tudor arch of an original hearth. A pair of bracketed side-shelves for tea and spices are small-scale versions of the mantel shelf that provides open storage for a cook's collection of pots. Baskets used to carry in fresh vegetables and herbs from the garden are suspended "out of the way." A painting overhead shows that there is never an inappropriate place to display art.*

ABOVE: *The rustic atmosphere of a ground-floor dining room suggests the style of an old English pub. A fireplace flanked by a matching pair of candle sconces, and a candle chandelier overhead show the owner's preference for firelight over electric. The plaster between the exposed beams of the ceiling is painted a deep red to complement the green color of the door, grandfather clock, and ceramic wall tiles.*

BEDROOMS, NURSERIES, AND BATHROOMS

Until the late Middle Ages, bedrooms tended to be a perquisite of the wealthy, and no piece of furniture was more coveted or more expensive than the bed. These beds were often massive wooden structures, ornately carved, and perhaps even bearing the family coat-of-arms. To provide privacy from servants who may have been sharing the bedchamber, and in colder climates to ensure warmth, the bed was often heavily draped with ornate tapestries or imported velvet, damask, or silk. In later eras, bed styles evolved to incorporate canopies, paneled or upholstered head- and footboards, posts, and other decorative elements. Today's English country bedrooms retain a sense of the past, with a fondness for canopies, draperies, and other bed hangings.

More than any other area of the house, the bedroom is designed to be a private space. In the bedroom, one is surrounded by cherished items that express one's most personal passions. The bedroom is a refuge from the busy world, a place to relax and shed the cares of the day.

English country style itself is all about comfort, so it is only natural that the English country bedroom is epitomized by words like casual, charming, and cozy. A wrought-iron, brass, or carved wooden bed, replete with canopy or four-postered and draped, provides the centerpiece around which the rest of the room's furnishings gather. Great attention is given to incorporating collections of fine bed linens,

layered for comfort and style, and topped with numerous plump pillows and cushions. Patchwork quilts, which may be family heirlooms, add unsurpassed country flavor. The mainstay of the English country look, mixed patterns and prints, manifests itself here in softly colored florals and stripes chosen for their gentle charm. Harmony is achieved in a unified decorative scheme of matching or complementary valances, curtains, wallpaper, and upholstered pieces.

Furniture in the bedroom is likely to include an armoire, as closets are rarely found in old houses, unless they were added at a later date; a chest of drawers, a trunk, and perhaps a small desk. Older wooden furniture that has fallen on hard times may get a new life from a coat of paint, stenciling, or a decorative paint treatment.

Accessorizing personal spaces is essential to creating an atmosphere of pure relaxation. Here, collections that are particularly

OPPOSITE: *Dual-purpose curtain panels on brass rods separate the bedroom from the bath and theatrically frame the large painting centered on the back wall. The generously sized white bed coverlet is echoed by the fabric draped over the bedside table round. Clutter has been kept to a minimum.*

precious may find the perfect site—cut crystal cosmetics jars with silver lids, perfume bottles, tortoiseshell hair-brushes and combs, antique shaving brushes—any of these might adorn a bedside table. Books, ubiquitous in an English country home, may be scattered casually or more formally arranged in scaled-down bookcases.

It was during the Victorian era that special care began to be taken in the decoration of nurseries and childrens rooms. Indeed, child-sized furniture and accessories are favorite collectibles among admirers of Victorian style. Today, an English country room for a baby might contain an old painted iron crib or pram, a white-painted wicker rocking chair, antique dolls or a dollhouse, and nineteenth-century prints. For a childs room, collections of toys and books, a painted wooden floor, and scattered throw rugs evoke the mixed-up comfort of English country without too much clutter.

The bathroom is a fairly recent addition to the house. Until the late nineteenth century, when indoor plumbing became widespread, people used chamber pots or outdoor privies; washing was done indoors using portable tubs or washstands. Thus, the bathrooms in older country houses have usually been converted from what were once small bedrooms or other rooms. As a result, bathrooms may be quite large, and include multiple windows, lots of space, and even a fireplace; or they may be very small. In either case, English country style can be adapted to create a charming bathroom, with floors of wood or tile, and wainscoting or pretty wallpaper on the walls, and incorporating old-fashioned accessories, lots of plush towels, colorful fabrics, and fresh or dried flowers.

A B O V E :   *Tongue-and-groove wainscoting surrounds a basic khaki and cream bathroom and encases a bathtub to hide its plumbing fixtures. Decorative elements not typical of bathrooms such as a mix of pictures, a black iron garden chair, and wall-to-wall carpeting show that the room is treated like an extension of the bedroom.*

A B O V E : *Architecture directed the decorating scheme of this handsome bedroom with Tudor-style wood paneled walls and a massive fireplace. The walls' rich brown is set off by white and beige bed linens and off-white carpeting, and is repeated in the furniture choices. The pale color scheme reflects the bright natural light generously provided by a long row of leaded glass windows and keeps the room from becoming dark and heavy.*

ABOVE: *A chic white plaster mirror framed with stylized scrolls is the focal point of this sparsely decorated bathroom. A simple porcelain tub with a hand-held brass showerhead is accompanied by an evocative Victorian wicker chair. The mirror reveals other interesting bathroom fixtures: a Victorian-style toilet tank and vanity.*

RIGHT: *Canvas-colored walls and curtains, and light, pickled floorboards allow disparate objects to work well together, like the red tropical fabric draping a chair, a heavy wood chest with a heraldic motif, and a zigzag rug of bright colors.*

A B O V E : *The well-worn but stately appearance of a master bedroom derives from the generous height of the ceiling and its massive window. Dressed with cotton chintz fabrics, the combination of patterns on the curtains, bed canopy, and upholstered easy chair creates an inviting refuge. The warming effect of the soft red fabrics is enhanced by the yellow-painted walls.*

ABOVE: *A daybed for sitting and sleeping was put in this room which was big enough to hold only a twin bed and little other furniture. Pulled together by a well-chosen mix of blue and cream chintz, the upholstered headboard and custom-made bed canopy and window curtains show that no element of the design was left unconsidered.*

ABOVE: *A sloped roofline is taken advantage of by the attached bed corona, giving the bed a majestic presence.*
A muted-color chintz fabric dominates the decorating scheme and pulls the room together.

OPPOSITE: *Striped wallpaper in two tones of gold enriches a bedroom of harmonious objects, colors, and textures. All-white bedding dresses the carved bed to set off its unusually carved headboard and provides a cool balance to the warm tones of the walls and furniture. An all-brown lamp and shade are well chosen to repeat the rich color of the wooden bed.*

ABOVE: *Blue and white porcelains and a sterling silver comb, brush, and mirror are classic embellishments of a skirted bedroom table. Set against a backdrop of floral chintz fabric, the objects represent quintessential English country style.*

OPPOSITE: *A comfortable bedroom's white walls and use of patterned fabric provide a domesticated setting for a restrained display of personal objects. Rows of pictures are neatly arranged according to matting color and size. The table top and mantel are employed as showcases for plates, postcards, small porcelains, and boxes of stationery. Daylight or incandescent lights are used to illuminate the family's collections.*

ABOVE: *A cornflower blue footed bathtub sits on wall-to-wall carpeting that matches the blue and white wide-striped wallpaper in a traditional country bathroom. Personal touches of silver-framed photographs, and cobalt apothecary and perfume containers add to the bathroom's charm.*

ABOVE: *A bathroom shows a Victorian penchant for clutter. A decoupage screen serves only a decorative function in its position between the bathtub and the wall. The clothes rack is hung with arrangements of dried flowers, also serving a decorative function.*

ABOVE: *This all-white rugged cottage bedchamber looks almost Mediterranean with its freshly painted walls and use of blue. Unfinished exposed floors echo the supporting lintels that are embedded in the walls and ceiling.*

RIGHT: *Next to the gilded side chair and built-in wardrobe, an English pine chest of drawers stores the overflow of a large collection of bedding. The chest blends visually with the more ornate pieces because of its unobtrusive design and simple lines.*

OPPOSITE: *A wood bassinet with fresh white linens and a protective mosquito net provides a nestlike cradle for a newborn. Dusty rose walls bring a warm and soothing quality to this nursery.*

RIGHT: *A child's room is casually strewn with antique dolls, miniature furniture, and stuffed animals. When streaming sunlight turns to moonlight, one can imagine that the enchanting nursery takes on a magical quality.*

ABOVE: *Floral chintz fabric covers this matching pair of iron beds and dominates the room's decorating scheme. Window treatments pick up the cool blue of the duvets and coordinate with gray-blue walls. A round-topped center table is dually shared for bedside reading material, a table lamp, and an arrangement of fresh-cut flowers that echoes the chintz.*

OPPOSITE: *A dormer window with a child-size windowseat was fitted with a curtain tailored to the hipped-roof alcove. Cool blue patterned walls bring airiness to the compact space filled with a young girl's toys and a china tea set on loan from Mum.*

OPPOSITE:
Decorated for personal pleasure, a bedroom can be a gallery that reflects a collector's love for artwork. An eclectic variety of subjects, styles, sizes, and mediums is hung in a balanced arrangement and positioned to give bedside viewers a good vantage point. Other cherished pieces crowd the tabletops below.

RIGHT: *In a lady's boudoir, a white-painted writing desk sits in front of a bedroom window for natural light. Framed photographs crowd every available surface, adding a personal touch.*

ABOVE: *Every inch of space is filled on the surface of a woven wicker side table. A traditional collection of blue and white Chinese porcelains, ivory elephants, and bowls of potpourri surrounds a colorful lamp with a fruit-and-leaf motif.*

OPPOSITE: *An iron twin bed sits opposite a small fireplace with a stylized Art Nouveau design. Curves are repeated in the bentwood Thonet-style rocking chair and complement the repetitive hard lines of the bed and the room's irregular walls and ceiling. Yellow wallpaper brings warmth to the oddly shaped space.*

LEFT: *A pale-colored bedroom glows with afternoon sunlight reflected off crisp white bed linens and curtains. The grouping of a variety of furniture styles works because of their carefully planned placement around the central bed and the light sisal carpet, cream walls, and white ceiling.*

ABOVE: *An irregularly shaped bathroom wall is enhanced by the display of different blue and white plates. A series of delft tiles surrounds the wall above the tub and continues behind the sink, creating a backsplash with visual interest. An old standing towel rack stores towels and serves a decorative function.*

ABOVE: *A romantic bedroom's decorating scheme possesses an air of restraint. Putty walls are a sophisticated balance to the feminine lace table covers. The bed covering echoes the look of real lace. The sedate color also sobers the bows that tie back the valances, and keeps the room from seeming overly fussy.*

OPPOSITE: *Exposed pine beams embedded in white stucco are the main attraction in this chalet-style upstairs bedroom. A single framed engraving hung just below the roofline is the only embellishment needed. The casually tossed bright-colored throw blanket stands out confidently among the essential furnishings.*

Part Four

AMERICAN COUNTRY

INTRODUCTION

What does a rough-hewn log cabin in Maine have in common with a pristine white Southern plantation house? Much more than meets the eye. The same holds true for a quaint Cape Cod cottage or tidy New England saltbox, lodgings that seem worlds apart from the squat adobes or low-slung Spanish colonials of the Southwest. Yet they are all kindred structures, for they are all part of the architectural vernacular that comprises American country style. This domain is undeniably as broad as the nation is big, embracing in its scope places to live and pieces to fill these places that are rustic and quaint, primitive and austere, or stately and poised.

American country encompasses elements from many different arenas because it represents all the diverse groups that settled this land. Each of these groups had different needs, different aesthetic legacies, and different skills, and their residences reflected these distinctions.

It was only natural for the first settlers to imbue their residences with elements that reflected their heritage. Thus, homes in the East tended to be based on forms familiar to that region's northern European settlers, such as the typical country cottages or farmhouses found throughout England, Germany, France, Holland, and Sweden. These designs eventually trickled farther west as the rest of the country was settled. At the same time, Native American and Mexican influences permeated the Southwest and made their way east. And what was inside each home followed suit: furnishings reflected the cultures and capabilities of furniture makers and artisans.

On the eastern seaboard, colonial quarters and accoutrements were heavily influenced by the English. The William and Mary, Queen Anne, Chippendale, Federal, and Empire periods were reinterpreted. Country craftsmen kept up with new woodworking techniques, though their creations tended to be simpler than that of their city counterparts: they often brought their own imaginative decorative additions to these designs. Thanks to these "amendments," rural styles that ran the gamut from rustic to ornate were born.

OPPOSITE: *A classic that came into vogue right after the American Revolution, this weatherboard Federal home has traditional details such as symmetrical six-over-six sash windows and a square-columned portico. The spread of this fashionable residential design in the last decades of the eighteenth century was related to newly arrived craftsmen from England.*

Similarly, the Germans and French who left Europe during the same period left their mark. The Germans, who for the most part settled outside Philadelphia, preserved their folk traditions with the same frothy, ornately embellished furniture they had left behind, while the major contribution of the French immigrants, who settled along the Mississippi River, was the armoire, a now-ubiquitous piece in any decor.

From religious communities such as the Quakers, Shakers, Amish, and Puritans, who settled in the Northeast and Midwest, came a form of country styling based on strong, clean-lined designs that were in keeping with the strict creeds that dictated their lifestyles. The homes and furnishings these groups produced were simple, plain, functional, and devoid of extraneous embellishments. Much of it is so straightforward and elegant that it is often emulated in minimalist designs today. Authentic pieces are coveted, and reproductions, especially of Shaker pieces, are routinely produced.

In the Southwest, design was influenced by Native American cultures and the Spanish conquistadors, who introduced metal hand tools to the continent in 1598 when they established the first permanent colony in New Mexico. Missionaries and Spanish *carpinteros* taught natives to build Spanish-style furniture and adobe dwellings. The missionaries also introduced the Spanish tradition of furnishing a home sparsely. In the mid-1800s, Anglo-American settlers started trickling into the area with their own design traditions. Today, these influences have developed into a distinct Southwestern style that combines elements from all three cultures.

RIGHT: *Most colonial homes were made of wood since it was more readily available, cheaper, and faster to build with than stone or brick, which were usually reserved for finer buildings. But German and Dutch settlers routinely built stone houses with low walls and deep roofs, such as this country cottage.*

ABOVE: *Barns, which came in many incarnations, were found flanking farmhouses as well as homes in smaller towns. Today they are often converted to residences, especially those that exist in more populated areas. Their rustic demeanor make them perfect candidates for creating a country-style residence.*

OPPOSITE: *Houses in the South were built with high ceilings, large windows, wide overhangs, and shaded porches to stave off the heat. They also had strict neoclassical decorative treatments, evident here in the Ionic columns on the portico. Porches based on classical temple portico forms were also quite popular on these homes, especially on those that anchored plantations, since they lent elegance and grandeur to a structure.*

Aside from cultural disparities, environment was perhaps the strongest factor to influence American shelters. Homes in the North and the heartland were designed to retain heat and withstand harsh elements, while those in warmer climates were devised with an emphasis on keeping cool. Hence a variety of well-insulated, cozy structures of wood, clay, stone, or brick punctuated with small, tightly fitted windows and large chimneys sprung up in the North, while homes in the South were built with high ceilings, large windows, porches, and courtyards.

And just as these structures and the effects that filled them were based on the heritages of their creators and on environmental considerations, they were also determined by the resources of the new land. Country craftsmen had to work with whatever materials were available in their locales, which usually meant indigenous wood, stone, and clay. This led to experimentation and alteration, resulting in a variety of new innovations and designs.

American country style was touched by social as well as historical influences. In the nineteenth century, both the Industrial Age and the Victorian mores affected this style. Thanks to the machine age, it took less time to make furniture and it was more affordable. But industrialization caused a backlash and created a nostalgic attraction to the preindustrial past. Decorating trends encompassed all sorts of furnishings that filled this calling, especially pieces that were rustic, romantic, eccentric, and sentimental, often made of exotic materials such as roots, branches, twigs, bark, and horn instead of wicker, cast iron, and wood.

Today, country style is not really about "the country" at all, but is, rather, a mind-set. It's comfortable, nurturing, and engaging—in essence, an alternative to hard-edged or sleekly orchestrated "urban" decors. And above all else, it's multifaceted. The style can be minimal and architectural, as the Shakers showed us with their pristinely crafted, spare interiors. Or it can be flooded with texture, color, and pattern, all cunningly employed to evoke moods that range from rustic and primitive to romantic and posh. In fact, the variety of elements and environments that qualify as country is nothing short of astonishing.

The humble hodgepodge is just as much a part of the milieu as the refined, carefully coordinated room. And provenance or purism are unimportant; tenor and spirit are far more significant to consider when creating a country interior than authenticity or period. Pieces can be reproductions or representative of different eras and styles; ultimately it is the mix and mood created with these accoutrements that counts.

The following chapters will show all the looks that comprise American country style and the many ways there are to achieve them. You can choose from a wide variety of furnishings, finishes, and surface treatments. And be creative when planning your design in this style—these ideas can be adapted to virtually any type of home.

ABOVE: *Door hoods were common in colonial times since they gave protection and decorative emphasis to an entry without the expense of a porch. Thanks to the addition of Doric columns, this hood has the aesthetic importance of a porch.*

OPPOSITE: *A one-room cabin was the typical home of a pioneer. Swedish settlers are thought to have introduced log construction to the colonies in the early eighteenth century, a method of building that became popular in rural areas. The cabins have small, tightly fitted windows and doors for protection from the elements.*

THE MIXING BOWL: DETAILS OF COUNTRY STYLE

Getting the details right is an essential part of creating a country home, be it cozy, quaint, primitive, or spare. And since the country interior has spanned the centuries in America, there's no need to stick to any specific period. The roots of the style come from our rural past when practical considerations rather than worries about beauty dictated the way a home looked. Elements that filled a country room were chosen for need, not want, and were rarely purist in ethic, so almost anything goes. Pieces from the colonial and Shaker periods are just as valid as Victorian- or Depression-era furnishings, and all of these pieces can be mixed at will in the American country interior.

Since there are no strict constraints about what works and what doesn't—and no rules and regulations to follow about what finishes, furniture, or fabrics constitute American country style—be creative. The materials that were employed to build a country abode, such as stone, brick, logs, and planks, are ideal for adorning the interior of a home and can be used on walls, ceilings, and floors. Pieces or effects from every era can be employed for furnishings. They can take the form of rough-hewn primitives, fancied-up antiques, or even contemporary pieces, as long as they are arrayed with a country sensibility.

OPPOSITE: *Simplicity can speak for itself, evoking a mood that's often impossible to achieve under other conditions. The austere bones of a room, especially if they incorporate architecturally significant details such as beams, sash windows, or paneled wood doors, can often stand alone with little accessorizing. A room can be transformed with a few powerful antique pieces, as in this example where a rustic bowl filled with woven fruit sits atop a gateleg table.*

Yet creating a country sensibility is perhaps the hardest part of the equation, for there are no hard-and-fast rules. Be aware of history and tradition, but don't follow them obsessively. Choose colors that have the earthy overtones exemplified by vegetable dyes and milk paints, but make sure they please you first rather than epitomize the style. Follow the same game plan with furnishings: pieces that fulfill your needs are more important than items that just look good. Finish it all off with decorative accessories that tie everything together or balance pieces from different periods. For instance, a contemporary cabinet can acquire a rustic ambience filled with a collection of primitive toys, and a group of framed samplers can give a plain plaster wall country appeal. Feel free to experiment, for trial and error is the best way to make it all work.

ABOVE: *There's power in numbers, as evidenced by these Shaker baskets, which make a much more powerful statement stacked in sets rather than displayed individually. Quilts folded atop the weathered blue hutch and draped in various places in the home further establish a country ambience.*

OPPOSITE: *A porch swing makes an unusual, eye-catching perch in the corner of a family room, giving the place solid originality. The house lacked a porch and the owners hit upon this solution so that they could swing their young children while reading. The "anything goes" spirit of American country style really comes across in this addition.*

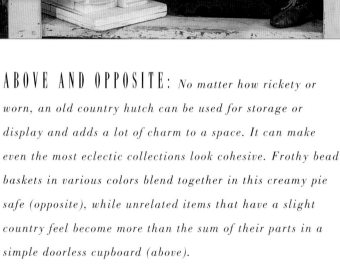

ABOVE AND OPPOSITE: *No matter how rickety or worn, an old country hutch can be used for storage or display and adds a lot of charm to a space. It can make even the most eclectic collections look cohesive. Frothy bead baskets in various colors blend together in this creamy pie safe (opposite), while unrelated items that have a slight country feel become more than the sum of their parts in a simple doorless cupboard (above).*

ABOVE: *The weathered front doors are the best attributes of this ancient hutch, so they've been left intact while the bottom doors have been removed to showcase collectibles such as decorative candlesticks, a tray handpainted with flowers, and a set of urns. Yet with still more to show, it makes good sense to use the top as a ledge for pitchers and teapots.*

ABOVE AND OPPOSITE: *The art of the tableau is just as much a part of country design as it is in any other style and can take many forms. Items may be different variations on a theme, such as these stars, which have been carefully arranged by color and scale to create an eye-catching display (above). Or they can be disparate and unique (opposite), combining elements both humble and grand unified by a carefully wrought balancing act to catch the eye and convey a country sensibility.*

ABOVE AND OPPOSITE: *Another way to highlight a tableau and imbue it with warmth is to anchor it with a source of light. The glow this light sheds on a setting will embrace everything it touches, and forges groupings of objects into cohesive vignettes. The burnished hues of antique woods come alive with illumination from a small table lamp, above, while opposite, collectibles on a worn, unfinished table are dramatically backlit against a window.*

ABOVE: *Every nook and cranny can be made interesting in a country home. Here, a porch is treated as grandly as a parlor with a picture hung right onto the home's exterior clapboard walls. All sorts of odd pieces come together here such as corn husks, a straw chair, and a wooden box filled with vegetables from the morning's stroll through the garden.*

BELOW: *A stairway goes from extremely worn to delightfully weathered with the addition of some well-chosen country collectibles. The pottery adds an earthy flavor while bright "watermelons" bring it all to life.*

ABOVE: *Upholstered armchairs were very rare in country homes because they were so expensive (their fabric was costly and they required the work of special tradesmen to make the frames and upholster them). But this cozy version looks right at home in a rough-hewn environment—proof that it's possible to hit just the right note between primitive and plush.*

ABOVE: *The rocking chair, one of the most familiar forms of seating in any home, happens to be an all-American innovation, with the first known examples dating from the 1750s. Just its presence provides an ample dose of country styling to its environment, not to mention comfort.*

ABOVE: *A rustic tableau takes on entirely new dimensions in this room awash in primary colors. Only a few appropriately colored accessories are necessary. The rag rug is purposely low-key to offset the room's vivid hues.*

THE KEEPING ROOM:
ONE GREAT ROOM

The early American country home consisted of little more that just one room, for resources—be they manpower or materials—were scarce. This room was officially called the "keeping room," and all the activities of a household, from cooking and eating to gathering and sleeping, occurred here.

Homes were humbly built out of necessity, but there was also a great deal of historical precedence for this simple floor plan. Provincial shelters in Europe had consisted of only one or two rooms. When the Industrial Age brought prosperity to such rural areas, the sizes of homes started to increase. The keeping room became less utilitarian as kitchens, storage areas, and bedrooms were added onto homes. This room ultimately vanished as separate living and dining rooms came into vogue.

Today, the custom of a country-style keeping room has come full circle, for a large, open space that blends meeting and eating areas is once again a popular component of the contemporary residence. In its current incarnation, the keeping room is known as the "great room." Yet the resurgence of this singular space couldn't be more paradoxical, since the prosperity that initially fostered larger residences with more rooms, and also begot today's hectic lifestyles, spurred the development of this latter-day keeping room. For like its forerunner, this space fosters the sort of intimacy and togetherness we crave today. And though it harks back to the keeping room, it is a thoroughly modern response to contemporary life; it is primarily designed to comfort us.

In light of such a calling, it's easy to understand why the great rooms of today are often arrayed with country trappings. We want them to attract and soothe us and we use wiles of the style such as ambient fires, cozy furnishings, and rustic structural materials to make us feel snug and secure. Fires call for mammoth hearths or earthy fireplaces that add warmth and soul to a room; cozy furnishings keep the space comfortable; and rustic materials such as muscular log beams, burnished wood paneling, weathered planks, or mottled bricks give the room character and depth.

OPPOSITE: *Decorative woodwork that is loaded with elegance and intricacies has its place in a country context, but is ultimately quite different in spirit from its urban brethren. Here a complex system of intersecting beams that is also carried over to the ceiling and walls of the room offers much more than mere structural support to the space. It feels rustic in tone, but is actually quite elaborate and creates a sophisticated system of wainscotting on the walls.*

Given the fact that these spaces combine several functions and the square footage of two rooms, they can also incorporate dramatic architectural or decorative devices, such as soaring ceilings or intricate millwork. Clad in country "garb," such as knotty plank paneling or gnarled log beams, or filled with country furnishings and collectibles, the great room ranges from relatively routine to remarkable. Thanks to all these options, the great rooms of today are usually all-encompassing spaces that have universal appeal.

BELOW: *A great room in a contemporary home gets its country pedigree from its trappings. Its enormous size is made cozy and warm with wood and stone. Furnishings play off the tones of these surface treatments. The burnished caramel of the pine paneling and cool blue-grays of the hearth are echoed in the room's upholstered pieces, which are prominent enough to fill the space yet grounded in simplicity. Octagonal porthole windows and a collection of vintage tools break the monotony of the expansive walls.*

RIGHT: *Architecture and materials— namely the wide-open plan crowned with a soaring ceiling and the stone hearth paired with rough-hewn log beams and walls—give this space its country legacy. The mood and spirit created by these devices is so strong that the actual process of decorating becomes less significant, as evidenced by the eclectic pieces used here. The Arts and Crafts table and rocker, an Oriental carpet, and a Queen Anne chair assume a rustic spirit.*

LEFT: *Even when designed in warm country materials such as wood and stone, contemporary great rooms can seem sterile and cold due to their vast ceilings. In this room, a network of intersecting rafters cuts the space down to more intimate proportions. It also serves to make the space far more interesting, since the wide-open expanse affords architects great creative leeway to devise structures that are "works of art" in themselves.*

RIGHT: *Nothing says "country" like a mammoth stone hearth and rough-hewn log walls and beams. The warmth and texture these elements dispense make them ideal components of an oversize room. They can make soaring spaces intimate as well as imbue them with country character, for virtually any decor can assume a quaint demeanor with these basics for a backdrop. And set against these architectural elements, pieces that are not necessarily country in pedigree, such as the deco-inspired furnishings here, can still seem pleasingly rustic.*

ABOVE: *Country styling can be rugged and elegant at the same time. Here, a craggy "physique" is outfitted in fine "garb," illustrating the point. The hearth and gables are clad in rough-hewn stone, and the rafters and cornices are crafted of coarsely cut beams. The gleaming floor and burnished furnishings are traditional and refined rather than rustic, though the room retains a country flavor thanks to its underpinnings.*

ABOVE: *British "club" style meets American country in this great room, where precisely tailored furnishings in paisleys and plaids are made less prim by weathered pine walls and coarse flagstone floors (as seen at left). The room also maintains a more formal mood, as the entertainment area is set off from the dining area by a sisal rug in buttery beige.*

ABOVE: *Although this vast great room has ample space for country collectibles, these pieces could easily become clutter if not presented properly. Quirky chairs are pegged to walls and kitschy odds and ends are set on the rafters to free up floor space and keep the room in order. Since wall space is at a premium, large, flat items, such as a caroms board and an advertising sign, are propped up against other pieces of furniture.*

ABOVE: *The inveterate collector who can't resist snapping up country artifacts can work a variety of them into the same environment with careful planning. Here, walls are kept pure white; sofas and chairs are covered in black and white checks or pinstripes; other furnishings are similar in hue; and like objects are tightly grouped together. Despite a profusion of pieces, everything blends together harmoniously.*

ABOVE: *There is no such thing as an authentic country-style sofa since upholstered furniture was rare in actual provincial residences (special craftsmen had to make them and woven fabrics were scarce). While the "shabby chic" or "colonial" styles have come to epitomize a country sensibility, there are other options. A boldly graphic quilt can turn any sofa into the star of the room, regardless of its style, as shown by the example above.*

LEFT: *Though great rooms tend to be more informal than separate living and dining areas, they can borrow a bit from both. In this version, well-edited country furnishings that are predominately Shaker in tone make the space at once casual and stately. A singular truss in the middle of the room is an architectural double entendre, paying homage to the traditional beamed country ceiling and setting up a subtle divider that still allows the room to function as one great space.*

RIGHT: *Thanks to multipurpose furnishings, the great room of this vintage cottage is exceptionally versatile. A chair-table tilts down to accommodate meals and can be moved away to be replaced by seating around the hearth. Though the chairs around the table are mismatched, they achieve a sense of unity because they all have box stretchers. Coincidentally, the chair-table sports the same design.*

LEFT: *A contemporary space gets a healthy dose of country styling with simple tongue-and-groove paneling and a stone chimney stack rising from an earthy hearth. Neutral upholstered pieces with high comfort quotients but no particular pedigree are joined with a rustic pine table and Native American rug to beef up the country ambience of the space.*

RIGHT: *Many wood-burning stoves do double duty: they provide heat and act as cookers. This stove anchors a true keeping room that supports many essential household functions. A conversation area in front of the stove has a low-slung table that can also be used for eating, while counters and a butcher block remain ready for culinary tasks.*

ABOVE: *When one room comprises the bulk of a cottage, it's important to make it engaging and versatile. Slipcovers are a quick, easy, and economical way to do so, and better yet, they don't have to be perfect to ply their charms. Sheets, textiles, or lengths of interesting fabric can work as well as, or better than, custom-made versions. Here, chunky upholstered pieces are transformed from ordinary to enchanting and inviting with simply draped sheets pulled over the frames in just the right way. Plump pillows make comfortable, cozy accents.*

ABOVE: *These wooden cabinets in disparate hues have been weathered to the same dull glow, coordinating with the room's plank walls and forging the perfect backdrop for the vivid fabrics. Though the fabric patterns don't match, they work well together because each one relates to a hue already employed on the cabinets. But the tableau isn't set in stone: two of the pieces (the chair and coffee table at right) are actually draped with sheets that can be changed at will.*

ROOMS FOR LIVING: SEPARATE BUT EQUAL

Once luxuries confined to homes in affluent cities, living and dining rooms are now very much a part of country homes. The true rustic cottage, which was built with just one or two rooms, acquired such formalities as it enlarged over the years. What was once the keeping room or kitchen became a living or dining room, which accounts for the massive hearths or brawny beams that grace many of these spaces. Newer homes, built in or since the nineteenth century, had separate living and dining rooms as prosperity spread to all reaches of the United States.

In the homes of today, country styling can be easily adapted to both of these rooms. And architectural provenance is relatively unimportant. Although it's nice to have burnished paneling, gnarled beams, rugged plank floors, or sash windows, a country mood can often be evoked, or teased out, with the right furnishings. Sometimes all it takes is one great piece, such as a rustic cupboard or a weathered harvest table. Often, country style can be achieved through a decorative paint treatment, folksy fabrics, or displays that show off whole collections of country artifacts.

Ultimately, though, the living or dining room that embraces country style strives to offer a cozy, homey environment that sets its occupants at ease. The living room is a space for relaxing with family or meeting with friends, while the dining room is at its best filled with guests sharing delicious food and lively, meaningful discourse. Given this calling, comfort and ease come first and dictate much.

Functional yet comfortable furnishings that aren't necessarily historical but elicit the right ambience are the most important elements of these spaces, such as cushy upholstered sofas and chairs, and large sturdy armoires for hiding contemporary electronic equipment in the

OPPOSITE: *A chair-table affords a room the utmost in versatility. Here it allows maximum use of a handsome hearth, permitting different activities to transpire in front of the fire. When open, it creates a formal dining environment, and when closed it can be moved to one side so the sofa and chairs can be pulled up to create a conversation area.*

living room and generous wood tables ringed with comfortable chairs in the dining room. Yet, it is often impossible to get authentic country pieces that possess these attributes because the necessary resources and skills weren't available in rural areas, and even when they were, they were on a far smaller scale than the pieces of today. The same holds true for the classic cupboard or armoire, which could never accommodate today's electronic equipment.

Hence these rooms can be filled with a wide range of furnishings, be it original or reproduction. The success of these spaces depends more on the careful blending of the formal and casual than anything else. Living rooms can easily incorporate new upholstery, just as dining rooms can be outfitted with a wide range of dining sets that will do the job. It's the overall environment these pieces help develop that is most important, and it can often be fostered by the way a room is arrayed with accessories. These are rooms to be lived in and enjoyed every day—not just on special occasions.

LEFT: *A contemporary space is graced with country flavor by the elements of its decor. A slim wood mantelpiece accentuates a small gas-flame fireplace, while a black-and-yellow brick pattern gives a folksy flavor to modern narrow moldings. Furnishings follow suit, with a mismatched rustic wood dining set; chairs and a sofa covered in a splashy floral print that evoke the sense of a cottage garden; and a wool dhurrie with a floral motif.*

LEFT: *Chairs of three periods (from left to right) Queen Anne, William and Mary, and Chippendale, hold court around a William and Mary coffee table and are given a unified demeanor by their dark wood frames and an Oriental carpet that defines the sitting area. The doors, door frames, and mantel are painted in soft shades of green to offset plain white walls and to make the space more inviting.*

RIGHT: *Wedgwood blue is hardly the color one would expect to see applied to paneling and rustic beams, yet it polishes this living room to perfection. The chalky finish imbues the paneled wall with a provincial overtone and plays off other elements in the room, such as the upholstery fabric, curtains, cupboard, and worn floor with its residue of blue pigment.*

ABOVE: *In true colonial form (for the term applies to a time frame that spans almost two centuries), this room blends pieces from several periods together. A Chippendale chair hovers in the corner; a contemporary Queen Anne sofa with charming stitched pillows skirts a wall; and reproduction benches, stools, a chest, and a cupboard that all pay homage to Shaker style fill the rest of the space. A true country feel is achieved, since the furniture as well as the accessories evoke a homespun early American mood.*

ABOVE: *The essential ingredients for a classic American country room are all here—a plump sit-and-sink easy chair, a well-worn leather sofa, a distressed wood coffee table, a painting of a rustic landscape, and wood paneled walls painted a dark green. Each of the elements alone may not necessarily say "country," but together, they create an effect of a refuge from a fast-paced life for the residents.*

RIGHT: *During the Federal period, walls of the finest rooms were papered with elegant scenery for those who could afford it. Preserved to this day, the picturesque paper imparts a quaint warmth instead of regal splendor on the living room. Curvy Queen Anne chairs upholstered with a flamboyant floral fabric are elegant, yet enhance the warm feel of the space and serve to soften the room's neoclassical elements.*

LEFT: *There's no need for purism to create a country demeanor: the style takes sustenance from imagination and daring. Here, a contemporary leather sofa, French fauteuils, an Empire cabinet, and a pie safe and wall hutch with true rustic pedigree set the stage for what could be a more formal space. But blooms rather than brocades cover the chairs, matching pillows transform the nature of the sofa, and the lush floral patterns of a huge hooked rug and valances give the space country styling.*

ABOVE: *Mini prints are particularly well suited to country homes, especially since their popularity stems from the very early days of printed wallpapers and fabrics in the eighteenth century. Here, a collection of small iron bells and kitchen and garden tools mixes particularly well with an intensely hued mini print, for both are equally dark and diminutive. Using the print on only some of the walls keeps the room from becoming too busy.*

A B O V E : *Windows everywhere keep the materials and hues of this room from feeling overpowering. Left beautifully bare, they let light spill into the room and bring the warm tones of the furnishings and finishes to life. There's clearly no need for window treatments in this rustic space as nature provides privacy as well as a verdant backdrop that tames the room's design.*

LEFT: *Wallpaper and paint can fill a room with style at a reasonable expense. A moss green wallpaper with a charming floral print, a clean white dado and molding on the walls, and a black-and-white check painted floor infuses this room with energy. Refined wood dining pieces in rich mahogany get a dose of country styling through these decorative devices.*

ABOVE: *Even polished furnishings, such as an intricately carved Victorian dining table and refined Viennese chairs, can acquire a country flavor. Here, a Depression-era hooked rug that sports a log cabin motif sets a distinctly country tone while other American country artifacts, such as art pottery with mellow brushed glazes and an antique Federal chandelier, strengthen the effect.*

OPPOSITE: *Chair-tables made sense in colonial times because residences were comprised of only one or two rooms that had to be multifunctional. But in a traditional dining room, the tabletop no longer has to be folded up when not in use—unless the owners want it that way. This type of table also presents an unusual dining surface, since a round shape is egalitarian and not common in rustic pieces.*

ABOVE AND RIGHT: *As these two distinctive yet similar spaces show, the same pickings can create a different presence in a room. The basic ingredients of these dining rooms are exactly the same—worn plank floors, six-over-six sash windows surrounded by plain wooden casements, colonial candlestick-style chandeliers, harvest tables, and Windsor chairs—but the result is far from the same. The stark lines of the comb-back Windsor chairs joined with strong terra-cotta walls and prominent contemporary art make one room (above) seem Shaker-spare and modern. But conventional creamy walls combined with traditional art, softer bow-back Windsors, a colonial sideboard, and a decorated fireplace and chimney stack create a warmer, more conventional feel (right).*

LEFT: *The sort of massive logs usually found in larger structures give this dining room—where bold trappings are employed in an unusually well-balanced way— lodge-style grandeur. Equally massive furnishings made of logs, planks, and tree limbs, which are in keeping with the Adirondack style of the room, complete the rustic picture.*

LEFT: *Two sides of country styling are revealed in this dining room where rustic meets refined. Dichotomous elements are paired together to stunning effect, such as gnarled log walls chinked with coarse plaster and polished pine panels crossed with an asymmetric design. Spare Shaker-flavored pieces that play to both the primitive and contemporary aspects of the room round out the setting and imbue it with timeless elegance.*

RIGHT: *Restraint keeps the pieces in this room from overwhelming each other. Almost everything is tucked away behind closed doors in the stenciled cupboard; the gleaming table is bare save for a fruit-laden basket centerpiece; textiles are kept simple with pinstripe chair cushions and modest gingham window treatments; and the walls are left mostly bare. A predominantly brick-red Oriental carpet plays off similar tones in the burnished furnishings and ties the elements of the decor together.*

LEFT: *Coarse plank and plaster walls are softened with sheer lace curtains, which add an aura of refinement and allow diffused light to stream into the dark room. While it would be difficult to adorn these walls with pictures, they are the perfect backdrop for storing kitchen implements such as baskets, pitchers, pans, ladles, and coffee mugs. Mix-and-match furnishings also work particularly well in this rough-hewn milieu. A rag rug is the perfect finishing touch.*

RIGHT: *A few well-placed, polished accessories can go a long way toward dressing up a rugged room, as shown here. Blue-and-white china plates grace a gnarled beam that serves as a mantel, and delicate creamy bowls and glass pieces adorn a wood table. A refined piece of art pottery filled with flowers makes for a lovely centerpiece and becomes the center of attention in the room.*

ABOVE: *A huge collection of printed Staffordshire china is shelved and hung on walls to show it off to fine effect. Boldly striped walls in a soft blue and cream harmonize with the blues found in most of the dishes, setting the collection off to perfection. An overflow of dishes tops a rustic sideboard, adding further dimension to the room by giving it a cozy Victorian tenor.*

COUNTRY KITCHENS: THE HEART OF THE HOME

The time-honored country kitchen has long been acknowledged as the heart of a home, and therefore, it should capture warmth, family life, and hospitality within its confines. This ambience can be easily achieved with earthy, humble materials that serve to counterbalance the sleek kitchen equipment available today.

With its charm and warmth, the country kitchen is the perfect antidote for our everyday chaotic lives. And the American country kitchen decor can be adapted to a wide range of tastes. It can be rustic and cottage-quaint or simple with rough-hewn splendor. Or, it may be fine-tuned to one of the many styles covered under the American country umbrella, such as Early American, Shaker, Adirondack, or Southwest.

But perhaps the main reason why country kitchens are coveted today and show up in so many residences is because of their practicality. In addition to the relaxed atmosphere these rooms exude, the materials used to achieve the look are hardy, economical, and utilitarian. Prosaic elements such as wood, brick, stone, or tile reign supreme and are cost-efficient, relatively indestructible, easy to clean, and only improve with age.

The country kitchen doesn't even necessarily have to be rustic, for the sensibility can be adapted to an urban or contemporary setting. Earthy materials can be blended with elements of high-tech or ultramodern design, adding warmth, balance, and intrigue to the room.

OPPOSITE: *A variety of rugged woods is often employed in country kitchens, since the woods will create an unpretentious and informal ambience. Here, a medley of woods, all worn with age and use, is responsible for the character, warmth, and appeal of the space. Other accents in this room that give the space its country appeal are baskets and pots hanging from the rafters and a quaint iron stove.*

Steel counters can top wood cabinets; open-wood shelving can hold the usual kitchen accoutrements and make a sleek environment inviting; and brick or tile can be installed on plain walls to provide them with depth and texture.

Thanks to such versatility, virtually any kitchen can get a healthy dose of country styling. Show off country collectibles or decorative accessories; furnish the space with rustic, primitive, or colonial pieces; introduce motifs with fabrics, tile, and color; or use surface treatments with paints or stains to modify floors, cabinets, and walls. If you're lucky enough to be starting from scratch, pave floors with planks, brick, or stone; craft cabinets out of wood; clad walls in logs, stone, or tile; and finish off the ceiling with an intricate and interesting support system made of beams or logs.

The country kitchen has come a long way from the keeping room. Thanks to the creativity and ingenuity we pour into the space, today it has become a "great room" in itself, for no other style of kitchen can be as inviting, flexible, utilitarian, and engaging all at the same time.

ABOVE: *British cottage styling comes to America with a crafty twist, for the traditional millwork in this kitchen gets a few modifications that pay homage to the eclecticism of this country. For instance, rail-and-stile cabinet doors have an updated decorative ring around their pulls, while open shelves are fitted with wicker baskets.*

RIGHT: *Hearths for heating and cooking were once the heart of every country home, but wood stoves assumed the same responsibilities much more efficiently in the nineteenth century. This iron stove is a secondary source of heat, but the image it conjures up is a primary design statement that's powerful enough to steep the whole room in country imagery.*

ABOVE: *Wood and brick may evoke the sense of a traditional country kitchen, but this space is anything but old-fashioned. Though the hearth seems primal, it's topped with a sleekly refined copper-clad flue that matches a state-of-the-art exhaust system, giving it an air of sophistication. The whole setup extends across a lineup of several high-tech appliances, which are creatively housed in rustic woods and gleaming black granite. The unusual blend of materials makes for a stunning and serviceable space.*

ABOVE: *A large kitchen in a new home gets its old-fashioned flavor from Shaker-style cabinets and sash windows with small panes. Rugged beams hung with herbs and dried flowers cut the space down to more intimate proportions. Classic country accents such as a blue-and-white plaid tablecloth, ruffled valances, a braided rag rug, dried-flower centerpieces in wood-carved "baskets," a candle-style chandelier, and a painted step stool round out the decor.*

ABOVE: *Too much of a good thing can be boring, which is why some of the wood cabinets in this kitchen have been painted a deep shade of green. Yellow ceramics play off a similar hue in the wood of the center island, while iron pans hung over the island complement the green paint. The result is a carefully contrived color scheme, which is highlighted with hooked rugs in similar hues.*

LEFT: *An element of surprise can shake things up a bit for the better. Here, a black-and-white checked tile floor, the epitome of urban chic, seems totally out of character with the country trappings in the space, yet it makes the room great by subtly playing off other elements of the decor: mellow two-tone wood cabinets; an antique pine cricket table with the same color value as the tiles; and decidedly rustic open-air shelves laden with crockery to counteract the urban influence of the floor.*

RIGHT: *Rustic trappings can coexist with high-tech appliances and soften the cold efficiency such equipment typically exudes. Here, a restaurant range is tempered by a sandy-toned tile backsplash, a stippled hood, and knotty pine cabinets that surround it. The refrigerator is cleverly masked behind a knotty pine façade.*

LEFT: *A few pieces of Quimper earthenware hanging on the back wall of this kitchen prove that a collection doesn't have to be massive to make a statement. All-white walls and a sweet lace liner on the ledge set them off. An old-fashioned range adds a sense of history, while the counter, made up of ceramic tiles hand-painted with flowers, has its own brand of country charm.*

LEFT: *A humble cottage kitchen goes from humdrum to exciting with a coat of barn red paint on its slat wood walls. The colored expanse lends country verve to the space, while an array of rustic trappings dots the area and garners it even more attention. Since the wood walls are one of the kitchen's strengths, it makes sense to highlight them. A twig bouquet and a hanging basket of corn, along with other country touches like a collection of teacups atop the molding around the door are perfect accents. Displaying utensils directly on the wall also makes the tiny area, which is very short on counter space, far more functional.*

A B O V E : *Simple wood shelves that span a wall organize oodles of dishes, glassware, and assorted odds and ends, but the turquoise cabinets below set them off to perfection. The secret to the success of this display is the sophisticated palette, for all the objects sport similar—and neutral—color values. The vivid hue of the cabinets draws the eye to the wall and brings the earth tones to life. Country collectibles on the unit's top shelf complete the setting.*

ABOVE: *An assortment of country accessories is unified through a carefully considered use of color on the cabinets and in the accessories themselves. If the wood cabinets were left unpainted, the kitchen may have been drab, but the combination of the earthy tones in the mixing and serving bowls above the cabinets and the muted pea green that covers the cabinets gives the room character and contrast.*

ABOVE: *It doesn't take much to dress up humble materials. Here, a deep shade of aquamarine paint calls verdant meadows to mind and gives finesse to plain plywood cabinets. A gingham valance and table runner, a gingham-and-floral swag, a tin filigree candle-style lighting fixture, a country-cute wallpaper border of apples applied at molding height, and a tile backsplash dressed up with hand-painted herbs give the kitchen a heavy dose of pretty provincialism.*

ABOVE: *A modest collection of blue-and-white transfer-printed china goes a long way in this kitchen, imbuing the room with loads of country charm. A stippled wall that mimics spatterware strengthens the mood, along with a frilly Victorian dining set, a snazzy black-and-white tablecloth, a wood spice rack, and a bucolic still life.*

LEFT: *Vintage stoves aren't specifically country in origin, but they do exude an old-fashioned aura that makes a great base in a country decor. Just a few true country trappings, such as a rack overflowing with well-worn pots, beadboard walls, and a quaint red-and-white table runner and rag-edged napkins over a brightly polished table strengthen the ambience but don't compete with the stove—a showstopper in its own right.*

RIGHT: *Long before there was refrigeration, baked goods were set to cool and stored in wooden-framed pie safes with elaborately patterned pierced-tin panels. Today, these are the kind of collector's pieces that can imbue a whole room with country charm. Here, just mimicking the coveted piece with a "pierced" refrigerator panel is enough to give the whole kitchen a country tone, as well as an ingenious way to diminish the impact of this huge modern appliance.*

LEFT AND ABOVE: *An eating area or breakfast nook off the main kitchen makes a perfect place to show off country collectibles. Stack rustic boxes on a sideboard, hang baskets from nails at the opening of the space, or take the door off a rustic cupboard to show off the contents, as shown at left. Or take one item and make it the center of attention. A bunch of country-cute tablecloths are layered on the table in the nook (above), while others were used to make cushions and upholster the fifties-era chairs.*

ABOVE: *The ultrarustic Adirondack log cabins and furnishings weren't part of the original country milieu, but were inspired as a reaction to growing urbanization in the nineteenth century. Designers created intricate homes and furnishings out of bent boughs, roots, branches, and twigs. Here, a dining set in the Adirondack vein teams up with a colorful diamond-patterned window border to liven up the spare eating area of a pure white beadboard kitchen.*

BEDROOMS: REFUGE FROM THE WORLD

At one time, rural families slept en masse in one room, which was also used for other activities such as eating, cooking, and entertaining. As America became more industrialized and our homes became larger, the country bedroom was born. If anything, it quickly became the most secluded spot in the home, for with the exception of this room, country-style homes usually feature open, communal, and multipurpose spaces geared to whole families. But whatever the country bedroom is furnished with, it follows one principle: it is not grand. This is a room where comfort comes first and governs every other consideration.

Not only is the country bedroom a haven today, it has retained many of the trappings from its first incarnation. For instance, the country bedroom may still feature a four-poster bed, which was originally draped on all sides for protection from the cold as well as privacy in communal environments. Huge storage cabinets or large blanket boxes also grace country bedrooms, holding spillover clothes and the like. Quilts that were often piled up to be used for warmth also have their place in the country bedrooms—and not just on beds. These quilts have proven to be the single most identifying mark of country style, often imbuing a whole room with warmth and rustic ambience, whether draped over a chair or hanging on a wall behind the bed's headboard.

OPPOSITE: *No item epitomizes the notion of American country styling better than the quilt. Given both the pedigree and appearance of this textile, which was begot by industrious and thrifty colonists who pieced together scraps of fabric in graphically imaginative patterns, its prominence as the premier country artifact makes sense. Introducing just one or a collection of many into a room will imbue the space with rustic ambience. It also counters the simplicity of spare country furnishings, bringing color and pattern to a relatively plain room.*

The country bedroom's four-poster bed can range from Shaker-spare to overtly ornamental and may or may not include a canopy. But these beds are rarely draped in full regalia today since drafts are controlled by central heating systems. Beds may be made of wood or metals that embrace a country sensibility such as brass or painted iron. Although the style of the bed sets a tone, dressing it to perfection may be the most critical aspect of furnishing a bedroom. This task not only makes the bed comfortable, but it gives the bed the allure needed to anchor the room. Making the country bed inviting and comfortable is often as easy as piling on plump pillows, thick quilts, and layers of crisp linens, all finished off with dusters and shams.

Storage is another important aspect of the country bedroom, and again the options are endless and easy to implement. Mammoth armoires and cupboards traditionally housed all of the effects of a household, but today they have become a staple in the country bedroom. They are coveted as much for their looks as their cubic footage, for they come in many varieties and are easy to find since antiques and reproductions of these pieces are plentiful. Dressers and chests are also available in old and new versions, and are often employed when the scale of a space prohibits larger pieces.

Given the flexibility and the endless options that can be explored for meeting storage and comfort needs, American country is a pragmatic, engaging, and easy style to employ in the bedroom.

ABOVE: *Country residents embellished their walls, floors, and furnishings with a wide range of designs by using stencils. Today these go a long way toward bringing a country demeanor to a room. Although sheer lace curtains, striped and floral wallpaper, and a wedding ring quilt contribute to the country charm in this space, the exquisite patterns on the bureau and bed are what imbue the room with true country styling.*

OPPOSITE: *A crocheted net covering draped across the curved canopy of this four-poster bed makes the perfect foil considering the large and dramatic nature of the piece. It not only coordinates particularly well with all the different textiles in the room, which include an all-white overshot coverlet, a calico patchwork quilt, a hooked wool rug, and sheer drapes, it doesn't fight the bold floral pattern on the wall.*

ABOVE: *Hand-loomed overshot coverlets are uniquely American, having originated in the eastern part of the United States in the eighteenth century. Originally made by women, these reversible textiles were eventually woven by professional male craftsmen who worked on looms they carried across the country. Overshots feature soft, heavy weft threads woven through a lighter background, in earthy shades of indigo blue, madder red, brown, and tan, and finishing touches such as elaborate borders or fringe are highly coveted in these textiles. Like quilts, they raise the country quotient of a room on their own, although they truly shine when paired with pieces in the same vein. This country bedroom that is purist in every sense is graced by a coverlet in primary colors that is complemented by colorful hooked carpets.*

RIGHT: *A cozy country bedroom makes the perfect retreat to be enjoyed at any time of day. The layout employed in this room creates two distinct activity areas: one for sleeping and the other for writing and reading. The chaise longue is perfectly positioned to take advantage of the room's inherent attributes, namely two windows that let natural light stream into the space. Hooked rugs with vibrant country themes separate the two distinct areas and make the open expanse the center of attention.*

RIGHT: *Antique wood pieces that derive great cachet from their authenticity are the focus of this small bedroom. A muted bed quilt, a rag rug, and a quilt suspended from a weathered green shelf that holds country collectibles punctuate the mellow brown tones of the furniture with texture and color, and help to brighten the room. A converted lantern is now a fixture, which contributes another dimension to the authenticity of the room.*

LEFT: *A hodgepodge of antique pieces, such as a colonial bed, an Empire chest of drawers, and a Shaker trunk, complement more rustic elements like a log cabin quilt and the room's rugged wood walls. The whitewashed plaster chinking between the wood planks plays off the creamy tones that dominate the quilt, and accessories have been kept to a minimum as the furnishings themselves are a bit bulky.*

RIGHT: *Quilts don't have to be confined to a bed or a wall. In this attic bedroom, a large collection of these and other textiles is displayed on the banister of a stairway, providing privacy as well as beauty. The plain rails go from utilitarian to ornamental, and the whole space takes sustenance from the texture and color of the quilts. And no detail has been overlooked: even the trundle is covered with a quilt.*

ABOVE: *Four-poster canopy beds originally had heavy drapes on all sides to both protect occupants from drafts at night and to provide privacy. But today, dressed in appropriate linens, they represent romantic country style at its best. It is important to outfit them in just the right way. Here, a bleached muslin canopy strikes just the right balance with the other elements of the room, which range from a daintily appliquéd quilt to densely patterned wallpaper.*

ABOVE: *Rag rugs, gingham curtains, and a pure white dust ruffle on a bed are the perfect neutrals to let rare finds, such as an intricate blue-and-white overshot coverlet and a stencilled Windsor settle, shine. Other aged pieces crafted in warm woods, such as a four-poster bed, a side table, a bureau, and a trunk, are handsome but unobtrusive, which strikes the right balance in the space.*

RIGHT: *Most authentic country beds don't come in contemporary sizes, but a bit of ingenuity can compensate for this. Here, a vintage wrought-iron garden gate from the turn of the century was made into a headboard for a standard queen-size bed. The bed, coupled with a vividly graphic quilt and a bright green cabinet filled with a collection of vintage sewing boxes, has given this plain white room a quaint countrified personality.*

RIGHT: *The right textiles can make a room. Here, a mix of sweet floral and gingham prints along with a hooked rug add cottage chic to a child's room. The fact that the fabrics are both old and new and are used in unconventional ways (such as for cushions on upholstered pieces and as double-sided valances) makes the mix more interesting.*

ABOVE: *A beautifully detailed bed can make a dramatic statement, whether it is a full-blown four-poster configuration or a sensible metal frame. Here, a painted white brass bed goes from slightly shabby to unabashedly romantic thanks to pristine linens lavishly layered with lace. The flowery wallpaper furthers the mood and adds a dash of sunny color to the room.*

ABOVE: *The informality of a country decor allows for lots of leeway. In this tiny attic bedroom, many distinct and eclectic elements are used to achieve a romantic mood, including a mint-hued balloon shade, intricate floral wallpaper, a painted bureau, and a boldly appliquéd quilt on a fancifully curved bed. Rather than fight for center stage, these devices harmonize thanks to their subtle tones.*

ABOVE: *A subdued green mural of rolling hills makes a relaxing backdrop for a room of rest, and coordinates particularly well with rustic pieces of furniture such as a four-poster bed, a fan-back Windsor chair, a provincial trunk, and oval Shaker boxes.*

ABOVE: *Beautifully carved box beds, which were enclosed on three sides and afforded their occupants privacy and warmth, were common in the European countryside. An "all-American" version is a perfect fit in this small log cabin. Built into a tiny alcove, this box bed accommodates two sleepers and affords lots of storage under each platform, creating a guest room with maximum privacy in a minimal space.*

LEFT, TOP: *A tiny attic guest room becomes an engaging multipurpose spot with careful planning. The sofa is situated on the wall of the room with enough ceiling height to accommodate someone sitting up, while the bed is tucked under the eaves. Painting the wood-paneled sloped ceiling white also opens up the small space. Finally, a patchwork quilt, a metal bed, and a wood chest give the small room its country demeanor.*

LEFT, BOTTOM: *Country style doesn't always call for purism. An ornate French sleigh bed and tailored English pine chest get a dose of pure Americana of the regional sort from an adobe hearth. The simplicity of the setting and a neutral palette help unify the disparate elements and make the room work.*

OPPOSITE: *A four-poster bed so strongly defines country style that its presence can give a contemporary loft the same brand of country ambience as a rough-hewn cabin. Although a few pieces, such as a wood bench and side table, further the country feeling, it is the linens, and especially a length of plain muslin draped horizontally over the frame, that reinforce the mood. This modern interpretation of the traditional canopy is cost-effective, easily installed, and a perfect match with the drapes over the mammoth glass doors in the room.*

SOURCES

DECORATIVE ACCESSORIES

Adirondack Country Store
252 North Main Street
PO Box 210
Northville, NY 12134
(800) 566-6235
Assorted accessories for the rustic home or camp.

The Chuctanunda Antique Company
One Fourth Avenue
Amsterdam, NY 12010
(518) 834-3983
Specializes in antique French and European enameled ware. Can be seen at major antiques shows and does an extensive mail-order business.

Country Curtains
The Red Lion Inn
Stockbridge, MA 01262
(800) 876-6123
Country curtains available by mail-order.

The Country House
805 East Main Street
Salisbury, MD 21801
Specializes in samplers, tinware, crocks, and other decorative country items.

Country Tinware
RR1, Box 73
Mt. Pleasant Mills, PA 17853
(800) 800-4846
Assorted candleholders, wall sconces, and lanterns.

Covered Bridge Quilt Supply
PO Box 333
Winterset, IA 50273
(515) 462-1020
Specializes in reproduction fabrics for quilts.

French Country Living
10205 Colvin Run Road
Great Falls, VA 22066
(703) 759-2245
(800) 485-1302
Specializes in French country–style decorative accessories.

Heritage Lantern
25 Yarmouth Crossing Drive
Yarmouth, ME 04096
(800) 648-4449
Specializes in wall and ceiling lights, sconces, and chandeliers.

Laura Ashley Home Collection
1300 MacArthur Boulevard
Mahwah, NJ 07430
(800) 223-6917
Specializes in fabrics and wallpapers.

Pierre Deux
870 Madison Avenue
New York, NY 10021
(800) 8-PIERRE
Specializes in French fabrics and accessories.

Rejuvenation Lamp & Fixture Company
1100 S.E. Grand Avenue
Portland, OR 97214
(503) 231-1900
Deals in reproduction lighting such as chandeliers, sconces, porch lights, Arts and Crafts fixtures, and Victorian-era lighting fixtures.

Renovator's
PO Box 2515
Conway, NH 03818
(800) 659-0203
Specializes in lighting, bath fixtures, and decorative items.

Restoration Hardware
Koch Service Road, Suite J
Corte Madera, CA 94925
(415) 924-1005

Royal Design Studio
386 East H Street
Suite 209-188
Cula Vista, CA 91910
(800) 747-9767
Specializes in stencils.

Arthur Sanderson and Sons, Ltd.
979 Third Avenue
New York, NY 10022
(212) 319-7220
Specializes in wallpaper.

Stulb's Old Village Paint
PO Box 1030
Fort Washington, PA 19034
(215) 654-1770
*Deals in vintage paint colors for
furniture, walls, and woodwork.*

Thibaut
480 Frelinghuysen Avenue
Newark, NJ 07114
(800) 223-0704
Specializes in wallpaper.

Yowler & Shepps Stencils
3529 Main Street
Conestoga, PA 17516
(717) 872-2820
Specializes in decorative stencils.

FLOORING AND RUGS
ABC Carpet & Home
888 Broadway
New York, NY 10010
(212) 674-1144

American Olean
1000 Cannon Avenue
Lannsdale, PA 19446
(215) 855-1111

Armstrong World Industries
PO Box 8022
Plymouth, MI 48170
(734) 331-7320

Bruce Hardwood Floors
16803 Dallas Parkway
Dallas, TX 75245
(800) 722-4647
Fredericksburg Rugs
PO Box 649
Fredericksburg, TX 78624
Specializes in rug hooking kits.

Charles W. Jacobsen, Inc.
401 North Salina Street
Syracuse, NY 13203
Specializes in Oriental rugs.

Karastan Carpets
PO Box 12070
Calhoun, GA 30703
(800) 234-1120

Mannington Resilient Floors
PO Box 30
Salen, NJ 08079
(609) 935-3000

Yankee Pride
29 Parkside Circle
Braintree, MA 02184
(800) 848-7610
Specializes in hand-hooked rugs.

FURNITURE
Baker Furniture
PO Box 1887
Grand Rapids, MI 49501
(800) 592-2537

Broyhill Furniture Industries
One Broyhill Park
Lenoir, NC 28633
(800) 327-6944

Century Furniture
Box 608
Hickory, NC 28603
(800) 867-0510

Cohasset Colonials
10 Churchill Road
Hingham, MA 02043
(800) 288-2389
*Specializes in reproduction Colonial
furniture, assembled or in kit form.*

Drexel Heritage
101 North Main Street
Drexel, NC 28619

Grange Furniture, Inc.
200 Lexington Avenue
New York, NY 10016
(800) GRANGE-1

Harden Furniture
8550 Mill Pond Way
McConnellsville, NY 13401
(315) 245-1000

LaLune Collection
930 East Burleigh
Milwaukee, WI 53212
(414) 263-5300
*Specializes in handcrafted willow
furniture.*

Maine Cottage Furniture
PO Box 935
Yarmouth, ME 04096
(207) 846-1430

Old Hickory Furniture
403 South Noble Street
Shelbyville, IN
(800) 232-2275
Specializes in rustic furniture.

Palecek
PO Box 225
Richmond, CA 94808
(800) 274-7730
*Specializes in bamboo, wicker, and
rattan furnishings.*

Charles P. Rodgers
899 First Avenue
New York, NY 10003
(800) 272-7726
Specializes in brass and iron beds.

Shaker Workshops
PO Box 8001
Ashburnham, MA 01430
Write for information.
*Specializes in reproduction Shaker
furnishings, assembled or in kit form.*

L. & J.G. Stickley Company
PO Box 480
Manlius, NY 13104
(315) 682-5500
*Specializes in Arts and Crafts
furnishings.*

Wellington's Leather Furniture
PO Box 1849
Blowing Rock, NC 28605
(800) 262-1049

Yield House
PO Box 2525
Conway, NH 03818
(800) 659-0206

KITCHENS AND BATHS
AGA Cookers
PO Box 213
Stowe, VT 05672
Write for information.

Crownpoint Cabinetry
153 Charlestown Road
PO Box 1560
Claremont, NH 03743
(800) 999-4994

Kohler Company
444 Highland Drive
Kohler, WI 53044
(800) 4-KOHLER

Kraftmaid
16052 Industrial Parkway
Middlefield, OH 44062
(800) 654-3308

Moen, Inc.
25300 Al Moen Drive
North Olmsted, OH 44070
(216) 962-2000

Plain & Fancy Custom Cabinetry
Box 519
Schafferstown, PA 17088
(717) 949-6571

Smallbone
A&D Building
150 East 58th Street
New York, NY 10155
(212) 935-3222

CANADIAN SOURCES

Au Courant
1100 Queen Street East
1100 Toronto, Ontario M4M 1K8
(416) 778-5547

Chateau D'Aujourd'Hui
6375 Rue Saint Hubert
Montreal, Quebec
(514) 228-4191

Christie, Manson & Woods Canada
170 Bloor Street West, Suite 210
Toronto, ON M5S 1T9
(416) 960-2063

Quintessence Designs
1222 Young Street
Toronto, Ontario M4O 1W3
(416) 921-3040

PHOTO CREDITS

Abode: 245, 248, 253, 260, 270, 275

©William Abranowicz: 66, 71 (designed by Denise and Michael Oppizzi), 79 top, 81 right, 82 left

Arcaid: ©Richard Bryant: 79 left, 84 (House of Marcel Proust's Aunt, Association of Marcel Proust); ©Annet Held: 64 ©Julie Phipps: 60, 223 right (Designer: Shirley Ann Sell)

©Philip Beaurline: 313, 341 top (Jeff Bushman, Architect, of Bushman Dreyfus Architects)

Corbis: 106

©Mitch Diamond/Photobank, Inc.: 42 left

©Edifice/Darley: 216–217

©Edifice/Jackson: 206–207

©Edifice/Lewis: 22 top, 44 bottom left, 196, 198, 209 right, 210 both, 214, 216 left

©Edifice/Norman: 30–31

©Phillip Ennis: 77 bottom (designed by Beverly Ellsley), 104 left (mural by Marlea Cashman)

Franca Speranza: ©Reto Guntli: 116, 117, 118, 173; ©Simon McBride: 124 left, 163, 175 bottom, 182-183, 188 top; ©Nider: 141, 149, 156, 157, 175 top, 180; ©Marina Papa: 121 right, 165; ©Paolo Sacco: 174

©Tria Giovan: 20, 29, 32–33, 34, 37, 38 (designed by Anna Thomas), 64 left, 64–65, 90 (designed by Charles Riley), 96 top (designed by Anita Calero), 101 right, 102 left (designed by Anna Thomas), 103 (designed by Anna Thomas), 104–105 (designed by Anna Thomas)

©Arthur Griggs: 36 bottom

©Steve Gross & Susan Daley: 301 right, 304, 306, 352 bottom (designed by Madonna Sullivan), 308, 309, 321 top, 324, 325, 342 bottom (designed by John Burroughs); 351 top; 352 top; 353 (designed by Gail Peachin); 359; 370 (designed by Hope & Wilder); 375

©David Henderson: 330 top

©Nancy Hill: 343 (The Country Dining Room Antiques); 302 (Jane Cottingham Antiques); 316 (Robert Orr & Associates, Architect); 317 (designed by Kerry Sheridan of Sheridan Interiors); 332 (designed by Diana Sawicki Interior Design); 338 top (designed by Helene Verin); 350, 351 bottom, 357 top (Kitchens by Deane); 357 bottom (designed by Margie Little)

©Houses & Interiors: 51, 69, 77 top, 81 left, 85 right, 105 right, 258, 265, 371; ©Steve Hawkins: 230

The Interior Archive: ©Tim Beddow: 200–201, 273, 277, 282–283; ©Simon Brown: 227 bottom, 264; ©James Mortimer: 229 (Designer: Stanley Falconer), 231 bottom (Designer: Steve Falconer), 266 (Designer: Stanley Falconer); ©J. Pilkington: 223 left (Designer: Jeremy Fry), 240 top (Designer: Lucy Ward), 256 bottom (Designer: Lorraine Kirk), 262–263 (Designer: Lorraine Kirk), 279 (Designer: Lorraine Kirk); ©C. Simon Sykes: 7, 224–225, 227 top, 228, 238, 255, 256 top, 278, 280; ©Fritz von Schulenburg: 203, 213 bottom, 215, 218 (Designer: Sam Chesterson), 221, 225 right (Designer: Emily Todhunter), 226, 231 top, 232 top, 233, 235 right, 236 both, 237, 239 (Designer: Emily Todhunter), 240 bottom, 241, 242, 249, 267, 268, 269 (Designer: Vicki Rothco), 285 (Designer: Emily Todhunter)

©Ken Kirkwood: 204, 208, 211, 212, 213 top, 222, 247 right, 250, 251, 252, 271, 272, 283 right

©dennis krukowski: 209 left (Designer: Tonin MAC Cullum, ASID, Inc.), 276 (Designer: Mary Meehan, Interiors Inc.) 293 (Rancho Santa Clara Del Norte); 312 (designed by Joanne M. Kuehner); 320, 344 (designed by Brenda Klein Speight); 321 bottom, 330 bottom (designed by David Webster); 334 (The Greenwood Farm)

©Massimo Listri: 122–123, 145, 155, 162, 170, 178

©Michael Mundy: 68, 82 right

©David Phelps: 2, 54 top (designed by Linda Chase), 56 left (designed by Linda Chase), 58 (courtesy First Women Magazine, designed by Lorraine Forenza, New York), 61 (designed by Linda Chase), 62–63 (designed by Linda Chase), 87 bottom, 91 both (designed by Linda Chase), 92 (designed by Linda Chase), 97 (designed by Barbara Levin Interiors, Inc., New York), 100 (designed by Dana Van Kleek, San Francisco, CA), 102 right (courtesy Family Circle Magazine)

Photonica: ©Kaz Chiba: 42 right, 44 top left

©Alessandra Quaranta: 130–131

©Eric Roth: 11, 15, 75 top, 75 bottom (designed by Elizabeth Speert, Inc.), 305, 339 (designed by Polly Peters); 307 top; 307 bottom (designed by Carol Harmon); 328–329, 371, 374 bottom (designed by Susan Zises Green); 338 bottom (designed by Kevin and Joanne Paulsen); 341 bottom (designed by Julie Alvarez de Toledo); 372; 374 top (designed by Carol Swift)

©Bill Rothchild: 48 (designed by Jeff Lincoln), 84–85 (designed by Teri Seidman)

Courtesy Rue de France: 38

Stock Image Production: ©Guy Bouchet: 17 right, 25, 33, 76, 88; ©J. Darblay: 44 bottom, 74 left; ©C. Dugied: 43, 73; ©Y. Duronsoy: 30, 31 right, 39; ©J.F. Jaussaud: 78; ©T. Jeanson: 60, 86 bottom; ©J.P. Lagarde: 12 bottom; ©J. Merrel: 45, 62-63; ©N. Millet: 85; ©C. Panchout: 49 left; ©C. Sarramon: 77 top; ©Terestchenko: 31 left

©Tim Street-Porter: 46 (designed by Bob and Isabel Higgins), 52 (designed by Annie Kelly), 56–57 (designed by Bob and Isabel Higgins), 59 right, 76 (designed by Bob and Isabel Higgins), 101 left (designed by McCormick Interiors), 161, 195 (Designer; Annie Kelly)

©Studio Giancarlo Gardin: 111, 112, 113, 124–125, 130 left, 132, 134–135, 136, 137, 138, 139, 142–143 both, 144, 146, 147 both, 150, 151 both, 152–153, 154, 158–159, 160, 164 top, 166–167, 168, 169, 171, 179, 184, 185, 186, 187, 188 bottom, 189, 190, 191, 192 both, 193, 194 both

©Angelo Tondini/Focus Team: 5, 10, 108, 114, 119 both, 122 left, 126 both, 127, 128 both, 129 both, 140, 148, 164 bottom, 167 right, 172, 176 both, 177

Tony Stone Images: ©Curt Fischer: 23; ©Suzanne and Nick Geary: 44–45

©Brian Vanden Brink: 7, 12–13, 286 (Willa Cather Home); 288 (Courtesy Maine Stay Inn); 290–291; 314 (Centerbrook Architects); 292; 294; 295; 296; 303; 310; 315; 340 (Bullock & Company, Builders); 322 (Jim Sterling (Architect); 323; 326; 333 top; 336–337; 347; 348 (John Martin Architect, Bullock & Company, Builders); 349; 363; 365 top; 367; 368; 373

©Dominique Vorillon: 79 bottom (designed by Jules des Pres), 99 top, 99 bottom (designed by Jules des Pres)

©Jessie Walker Associates: 50, 63 right, 78, 80, 89 right, 299 , 300, 333 bottom, 337 right, 358 right, 369 both (home of collector Katherine Garland)

Elizabeth Whiting & Associates: 8, 14, 220; ©Peter Aprahamian: 257; ©Nick Carter: 232 bottom (Designer: Amanda Baird); ©Michael Dunne: 274; ©Brian Harrison: 202 (Designer: Giles Wyatt Smith); ©Dennis Stone: 284; ©Simon Upton: 234–235 (Designer: Thelma and Johnny Morris), 246–247 (Designer: Robin Parish), 254; ©Andreas von Einsiedel: 244, 261

Leo de Wys Inc.: ©Mike Busselle: 26–27; ©de Wys/TFL: 24, ©de Wys/Sipa/Soren: 39 left; ©Fridmar Damm: 21; ©John Miller: 36 top; ©Jean Paul Nacivet: 18, 39 right; ©Steve Vidler: 16, 120–121